D1107815

TWAYNE'S WORLD AUTHORS SERIES

A Survey of the World's Literature

Sylvia E. Bowman, Indiana University

GENERAL EDITOR

SWEDEN

Leif Sjöberg,
State University of New York, Stony Brook

EDITOR

Eyvind Johnson

(TWAS 150)

TWAYNE'S WORLD AUTHORS SERIES (TWAS)

The purpose of TWAS is to survey the major writers—novelists, dramatists, historians, poets, philosophers, and critics—of the nations of the world. Among the national literatures covered are those of Australia, Canada, China, Eastern Europe, France, Germany, Greece, India, Italy, Japan, Latin America, New Zealand, Poland, Russia, Scandinavia, Spain, and the African nations, as well as Hebrew, Yiddish, and Latin Classical literatures. This survey is complemented by Twayne's United States Authors Series and English Authors Series.

The intent of each volume in these series is to present a critical-analytical study of the works of the writer; to include biographical and historical material that may be necessary for understanding, appreciation, and critical appraisal of the writer; and to present all material in clear, concise English—but not to vitiate the scholarly content of the work by doing so.

Eyvind Johnson

By GAVIN ORTON
University of Hull

Twayne Publishers, Inc. : : New York

Preface

Although Eyvind Johnson is recognized as one of the foremost Swedish novelists of the day, his countrymen have been reluctant to write about his work. Only one previous book on Johnson has been published, and that by a Dane, twenty years ago. Unfortunately, it is marred by the author's tendency to Danicize his Swedish quotations, and Swedish is to Danish as Oscar Wilde claimed music to be to German: "Whatever music sounds like, I am glad to say that it does not sound in the smallest degree like German." In writing this book I have borne in mind the shortage of critical studies of Johnson's works, and though I have tried to make the subject comprehensible to a non-Swedish, non-specialist public, I hope that Swedish readers also will find something new here.

The greater part of the book is devoted to a critical analysis of Johnson's novels, and the analysis is directed principally at revealing the ideas that lie beneath the surface of the stories—for Johnson, it seems to me, is above all a novelist of ideas. I have in passing taken up other points that seemed interesting, such as points of language, construction, and influence, but I have obviously been limited by the need to approach questions of style through translations. I am aware that by concentrating on ideas I may have made Johnson's novels sound even more dessicated than they are sometimes reputed to be, but then this book is merely a guide for the inquisitive, and possibly a commentary for the puzzled. It is not a substitute for the works it describes.

Quotations from Johnson's works are my own translations, and the page references are to the first Swedish editions. The notes and references at the end of the book are aimed particularly at those who read Swedish and want to extend their knowledge of Johnson beyond the frontiers of this study, in other works. I have *not* tried to conceal any of my arguments in the notes, and the ordinary reader may cheerfully ignore them.

GAVIN ORTON

University of Hull

Contents

Chronology

1900 Olof Edvin Werner Jonsson, son of Olof and Cevia Jonsson, born July 29 near Boden, Sweden. Brought up mainly by foster parents, Anders Johan and Amanda Rost.

1913 Left school. Moved with foster parents from Boden to Näsberg.

1914 Left foster parents. Started work at timber boom.

1914– Various jobs in Norrbotten.
1919

1919 Moved to Stockholm. Unemployed.

1920 Contributor to *Vår Nutid (Our Present)*.

1921 Emigrated to Germany. Lived mostly in Berlin.

1923 Returned to Sweden.

1924 *The Four Strangers* published.

1925 Returned to Berlin. *Timans and Justice* published.

1925– Living in or near Paris.
1930

1927 Married to Aase Christoffersen (deceased 1938). *Town in Darkness* published.

1928 *Town in Light* and *Remembering* published.

1929 Brief return to Sweden. *Commentary on a Falling Star* published.

1930 Permanently returned to Sweden. *Farewell to Hamlet* published.

1932 *Bobinack* and *The Night Has Come* published.

1933 *Rain at Dawn* published.

1934 *Once More, Captain* published.

1934– *The Novel about Olof* published.
1937

1938 *Night Maneuvers* published.

1939– Wartime activities: raising support for resistance to invasion of
1945 Finland, then Denmark and Norway. (1942–45 *A Handclasp*).

1940 Married to Cilla Frankenhaeuser. *The Secure World* and *The Soldier's Return* published.

1941– *Krilon* published.
1943

1946 *The Swell on the Beaches* published.

1947– Living in Switzerland.
1949

1949 *Dreams of Roses and Fire* published.

1949– Living in England: working for British Broadcasting Corporation.
1950

1951 *Put Away the Sun* published.
1952 *Return to Ithaca* published in London and New York. (Orig. published in 1946.)
1953 *Romantic Tale* published.
1955 *The Course of Time* published.
1957 Elected member of the Swedish Academy. *The Clouds over Metapontion* published.
1960 *The Days of His Grace* published.
1961 Visit to Greece. *Traces past Colonos* published.
1962 Awarded the Nordic Council Literature Prize.
1964 *Life's Long Day* published.
1968 *Favel Alone* published.

CHAPTER 1

A Man of the People

E YVIND Johnson was born on July 29, 1900, on the outskirts of what is now the city of Boden, in Sweden's most northerly province, Norrbotten. Boden was important as a railroad junction, where the line from Stockholm to the north of Sweden joined the then recently completed iron-ore railroad which runs between the ports of Luleå and Narvik, past the ore mountains of Lapland. The railroad was the reason that Johnson's parents were in Boden, for his father—Olof Jonsson—came from the western province of Värmland and his mother from the province of Blekinge, in the far south.[1] Olof Jonsson had come north as a *rallare,* one of an independent but close-knit body of laborers that built railroads across the most desolate wastes of Western Europe.

In his thirties Johnson was to write that the memory of his childhood could still depress him; not so much the memory of the long arctic winter as of a family tragedy—his father's illness: "I am told that he sang, that he was a cheerful and genial man, and I am happy to believe it. But he fell ill, he was ill for many years, and I never heard him sing. I scarcely heard him speak."[2] This mental illness resulted in his father's withdrawing into himself and being unable to work, and the family was reduced to poverty. The young Eyvind, then about four years old, was handed over to foster parents: his mother's childless sister Amanda and her husband Anders Johan Rost, a former fellow worker of Eyvind's father. Although the Rosts only lived across the road, Eyvind felt separated from his family: "When I was small I went home every day, it was nearby. I wanted to be with the others, be like them. I belonged there and I didn't want to be better off. I was intensely homesick all my childhood; when I finally came home I wanted to leave."[3]

Johnson attended the village school until just before his thirteenth birthday; this was the only formal education he has ever had. He then moved north with his foster parents to a lonely spot about forty-five miles up the line from Boden, a wilderness of marsh and mosquitoes in summer and snow in winter, with the railroad as the only link with the rest of the world. In June, 1914, Johnson decided he had had enough and left his foster parents. For the next five years he moved about the province of Norrbotten in a variety of jobs, starting at a timber-sorting boom, progressing to a brick kiln, working in a sawmill, operating a movie projector, laying drain pipes. He reacted to these experiences by reading a great deal, as a form of escape, and by joining workers' organizations, in an attempt to improve working conditions. In 1917 he joined the Boden branch of the Syndicalist section of the trade union movement, and for a time he was its secretary: his minutes are still preserved.[4] He also became a Young Socialist, thus showing sympathy with a movement that in its leanings towards anarchism lay well to the left of the mainstream Social Democrats. While the Young Socialists placed great faith in economic revolution, they also believed in the cultural education and emancipation of the proletariat, and their newspaper *Brand* encouraged literary contributions. When Johnson escaped from Norrbotten to Stockholm in 1919, he made contact with the Young Socialists in the capital and was from 1919 to 1924 a regular contributor to *Brand* of rousing articles and revolutionary poems, under the name of Eyvind Ung ("Eyvind Young").[5]

Johnson was not, however, to pursue his development within a political framework; his restless temperament took him his own peculiar way. His revolutionary faith was undermined by a tendency towards despair and nihilism. He has himself traced this to his experiences of the First World War: "We saw most clearly the worst sides of our fellow men: how in the heat of the world conflagration the most wretched qualities of man—desire for profit, coarse desire for pleasure, vanity, greed, and cowardice— put forth buds and blossomed like tropical plants."[6] His faith in man was further weakened by his discovery that when it came to a strike the solidarity of the proletariat was a myth: "I suddenly felt that the world was crawling with proletarians who personally didn't satisfy the slightest demands."[7] Finally, he suffered the aches and pains of disappointed love, private problems that tended to distract his attention from more abstract sufferings.

All this happened in Norrbotten, but things did not improve in Stockholm. Johnson found himself unable to get a job, and he was eventually forced to write to make money—a way of earning a living that seemed shameful to him.[8] He came into contact with other young socialists and writers, and they used to meet and argue in a cafe called "Fällan."[9] One particular friend Johnson acquired was Rudolf Värnlund, a friendship that lasted until Värnlund's death in 1945 and in a sense survives in Johnson's continuing defense of his memory. Värnlund was one of the driving forces behind a short-lived periodical the young writers produced called *Vår Nutid (Our Present,* 1920), which ran to no more than six issues. Johnson's romantic tales from Norrbotten scarcely reveal a great writer in the making. Yet again personal restlessness intervened, again Johnson had to escape: "I suddenly realized that I was faced with a choice: of either sinking down into a lousy bohemian existence or freeing myself in some way or other, quickly, with one blow."[10]

In October, 1921, Johnson left Stockholm as a stowaway on a ship bound for Germany. He was to spend the greater part of the next ten years on the Continent, first in Berlin, then in Paris. The Berlin to which Johnson came was a place of human misery and political and artistic ferment. Through his political connections Johnson came into contact with the world of Kokoschka and Ernst Toller.[11] He also met political refugees whose beliefs and actions had compelled them to flee west: "I met many strange existences, whirled up like scraps in the world whirlwind, and that was most fruitful. They were living documents in the history of the times."[12] In the fall of 1923 Johnson returned temporarily to Sweden, where he wrote his first book, a collection of four short stories published as *De fyra främlingarna (The Four Strangers,* 1924). He also began writing a novel, *Timans och rättfärdigheten (Timans and Justice,* 1925), in which he incorporated some of his experiences from Berlin. By the time this novel was published Johnson was back on the Continent, in Paris, and there he spent the next five years, often in extreme poverty, subsisting on the meager payments he received from Sweden for newspaper articles, short stories, and novels. His emotional mood swung from the idea of further flight—to Sumatra, this time—through love to marriage in 1927, back to despair at the death of his younger brother in America; all the while his literary education proceeded steadily, until he emerged as the most sophisticated and international Swedish novelist of his generation, with a fund of experiences that he is still drawing on today.

One particular experience that recurs in several of Johnson's

novels is a trip he made to the Bay of Biscay at the beginning of
1926: "Down there I discovered The Sea more than ever before
or since. The breakers rolled in from Biscay and broke in high,
wandering walls of water on the endless sandy beaches. I often
walked there, listened and observed."[13] It was there he wrote his
second novel, *Stad i mörker* (*Town in Darkness,* 1927), set in the
arctic winter of Norrbotten. The sea surges through this novel as a
longing for freedom and escape from the suffocating air of human
society, but the book ends with something like acceptance of,
or at any rate compromise with, this society, the town in darkness.
One critic sees in the story a reflection of a tempering of Johnson's
anarchist beliefs in the direction of parliamentarianism.[14] There
is, however, rather less sense of social solidarity in a contrasting
novel written shortly afterwards—*Stad i ljus* (*Town in Light,*
1928)—where a lonely Swedish author wanders through a festive Paris, seeing it all from the outside.

Before either of these novels was published Johnson had experienced the "explosion in the heart"[15] that led to his marriage,
and in October, 1927, he and his wife moved to Saint-Leu-la-
Forêt, outside Paris. Looking back, Johnson sees this as a turning
point in his life,[16] the beginning of a period of "family happiness,
happiness in work, calmer breathing," but also "other things concerned with death and grief."[17] The death was that of his younger
brother, in America, and Johnson's grief seems to have been considerable. It is reflected in the bitterness of his next novel, *Minnas* (*Remembering,* 1928), in which the younger of two half-brothers is brutally and meaninglessly murdered. This novel had started some time
earlier under a different title, and part of it had been set in heaven:
"When the author sent the manuscript to the publisher he removed
the Kingdom of Heaven in the probably justified belief that such
a heaven would not be appreciated. More earthly pages were
omitted at the same time."[18] Some of these omitted pages were
later incorporated in *Spår förbi Kolonos* (*Traces past Colonos,*
1961). In its original form *Remembering* would have been Johnson's
first important attempt to break away from the realistic novel
to achieve the mixture of reality and fantasy that is now the distinguishing feature of his work. *Remembering* was followed by
an equally bitter and disillusioned, if technically very advanced,
novel called *Kommentar till ett stjärnfall* (*Commentary on a Falling
Star,* 1929).

Fortunately Johnson was able to escape from the rather restricted vision of human achievement that cynicism provides: "In *Avsked till Hamlet* [*Farewell to Hamlet*, 1930], written after a short visit to Sweden, I seemed to see a way. It was a liberation from the state of affairs after *Commentary*, and in a way a continuation . . . . I again tried consciously to become involved in the wider scheme of things."[19] He reaffirmed his solidarity with the working class and his participation in their struggle, represented by the Russian Revolution. He also saw confirmation of a new spirit in the world in the works of Corbusier. When Johnson finally returned to Sweden in 1930, he arrived in time for the Stockholm Exhibition, which marked the breakthrough of Functionalism in Sweden. Johnson was greatly impressed: "The homecomer's most powerful impression of the exhibition was joy, a feeling of liberation and—however strange it may sound to many ears now—the beauty and purity of Functionalism."[20] This sense of joy and of liberation from gloomy concepts from the past, not only in building but also in living, is the theme of *Bobinack* (1932)—a curious given name taken from a fairy tale Johnson had come across in his childhood[21]—and *Regn i gryningen* (*Rain at Dawn*, 1933).

While Paris may have been the center of things from a literary point of view, for a Swede like Johnson it must have been a place of personal isolation. Back in Stockholm he made up for his exile: "I met my best friends, made new ones, I was hungry for company."[22] One particular consequence of the Stockholm Exhibition was the founding of a discussion group, of which Johnson was a member—"Trettonklubben" ("The Group of Thirteen"). At the meetings of this club "one member of the group would orient the others in a question, put forward a point of view about an event, give an account of some situation. A conversation, often lively, began; the perspectives were widened from Stockholm to the rest of the country and from Sweden to the world."[23]

For some time Johnson had been writing short stories with themes from his childhood province of Norrbotten; some of these stories, masterpieces in the genre, were published in book form in *Än en gång, kapten* (*Once More, Captain*, 1934) and *Den trygga världen* (*The Secure World*, 1940). Johnson showed that he could use his childhood memories equally successfully in novel form, in the tetralogy *Romanen om Olof* (*The Novel About Olof*, 1934–37). It is the story of an adolescent in much the same situation as the young Johnson had been, and it traces his development from his leaving his foster parents at the age of thirteen to his leaving Norrbotten altogether five years later. It is not, however, so much autobiography as an autobiographical novel.[24] It has recently been made into an award-winning film, *Här har du ditt liv* (*Here You Have Your Life*, 1966), by Jan Troell, who creates an extraordinary sense of the atmosphere of Norrbotten.

"The Secure World"—in 1940 the title was meant ironically, for while Sweden progressed steadily and peacefully towards the affluent welfare state, the rest of Europe was anything but secure. Johnson, with his inevitably internationalist outlook and his socialist beliefs, was well aware of the nature of fascism, but he was less certain what to do about it. He had always professed pacifism, and he had considerable doubts about the values represented by Western capitalist societies. But the situation was rapidly becoming one of capitalist democracies versus the totalitarian states of Russia and Germany. Johnson came to feel that the democracies, however imperfect they might be, at least offered the *possibility* of development—a possibility that did not exist in a totalitarian state, with its rigid suppression of discussion and debate. He also came to feel—with the greatest reluctance—that this possibility must ultimately be defended by force. Johnson's determined opposition to the expansionist policies of Hitler and Stalin was always qualified by the belief that force could only be used in the last resort, and that its use was inherently evil. As he declared after the war: "In my youth I belonged to a group in the working-class movement that considered that we should not kill people. *I still feel solidarity with this group.* The appearance of Nazism has changed my opinion somewhat about how and where we should use force. We must defend ourselves against a state devoted to force. But if we begin to see force generally as a moral asset . . . then not only those of us alive now but generations of men following us are ruined, lost."[25] Johnson argued that the only course for small nations like Sweden to puisue was one of solidarity with other small nations, for together they would be strong. He was a member of the group that published the newspaper *Nordens Frihet* (*Scandinavia's Freedom*, 1939–45) and argued that the Scandinavian states should pursue a common policy. Events disappointed them. When Russia invaded Finland in 1939, the other states refused to intervene, and when Norway and Denmark were occupied by the Germans,

Sweden remained neutral. Johnson did what he could as an author. He was the man legally responsible for the Norwegian Resistance newspaper *Et Håndslag* (*A Handclasp*, 1942–45), for which he wrote the leading articles; another regular contributor was a Norwegian of German extraction, Willy Brandt—later Chancellor of West Germany.[26] Even in such propaganda material Johnson expressed his distress at the destruction and suffering that the Allied air raids on Germany necessarily entailed.

Johnson's opposition to totalitarianism also dominates his novels from this period. *Nattövning* (*Night Maneuvers*, 1938) is the story of a pacifist who decides to join the International Brigade and defend the Spanish Republic against Franco; it is also a warning of fifth columnists inside Sweden. *Soldatens återkomst* (*The Soldier's Return*, 1940) is a tribute to the soldiers who fought on the battlefields of Spain, Finland, and Norway, in defense of democracy. More important than these two novels is the enormous *Krilon* trilogy (1941–43), which starts from the story of a discussion group rather like "Trettonklubben" and expands into "a complete picture of the world as I myself saw it."[27] It is an account of man's eternal struggle against evil, and more particularly of the Allies' struggle against Nazism. The novel is an extraordinary mixture of realism, allegory, fantasy, symbolism, and not least journalism. This last quality is exemplified by one incident. In March, 1942, seventeen Swedish newspapers were seized by the police because they included reports of torture by the Gestapo in Norway—reports that could endanger Sweden's attempts to placate Hitler. Johnson duly published extracts from these reports in the second volume of the trilogy, and then tongue-in-cheek reported the seizure of the newspapers in the third volume.[28] It is not only the Swedish government that is the target of the murderous satire in the novel. A critic and Buchmanite who had attacked Johnson's defense of Western democracy as hypocritical is devastatingly ridiculed in the character of Tollius. *Krilon* is a thoroughly contemporary novel, populated by real live personalities from Sweden of the 1940s—including self-mocking glimpses of the author himself. In *Strändernas svall* (*The Swell on the Beaches*, 1946) Johnson approached the subject of the Second World War through the medium of Homer's *Odyssey*. Homer was an old companion of Johnson's. He had first read him in Boden[29]; and in difficult moments in the 1920s Homer was a source of strength and consolation.[30] On the shores of the Bay of Biscay he felt that he had found Odysseus's coast, and he even met Odysseus, a naval captain who told him strange tales of the places he had visited. [31] Men, Johnson seems to say, are much the same in all ages of history; it is only the external details that are different. The events and emotions of the historical past are a reflection of contemporary situations. *The Swell on the Beaches* discusses the soul-searching of Odysseus before he kills the suitors, and the problems are little different from those of the pacifist in *Night Maneuvers* who takes part in the Spanish Civil War. That is why *The Swell on the Beaches* can bear the subtitle "A Novel about the Present."

Johnson's postwar works are characterized by a sense of history. He uses historical themes not only because they present parallels to contemporary events but also because understanding the present involves understanding the past: "No one period of time on its own forms our present. I mean, the experiences of the past mingle with our daily life, the daily life of those now living, just as our present, what is present at the moment, will in its way mingle with the life of the future."[32] This doctrine is illustrated by four historical novels: *Drömmar om rosor och eld* (*Dreams of Roses and Fire,* 1949), about the burning of a priest for witchcraft in seventeenth-century France; *Molnen över Metapontion* (*The Clouds over Metapontion,* 1957), in part a retelling of Xenophon's *Anabasis;* *Hans nådes tid* (*The Days of His Grace,* 1960), set in the Europe of Charlemagne; and *Livsdagen lång* (*Life's Long Day,* 1964), a mixture of several historical tales. Johnson's historical sense has been nourished by his frequent visits to the European continent and his contact with the monuments of past civilizations and the scenes of much of European history.[33] He lived for some time in the canton of Graubünden in Switzerland (1947–49), reporting his observations in *Dagbok från Schweiz* (*Diary from Switzerland,* 1949).[34] And he then spent a year in England, describing his impressions in articles that, as always, emphasize the literary and historical nature of his observations.[35] The distance—and yet proximity—that history lends his stories seems ideally suited to Johnson's temperament, and these historical novels are the high-watermark of his achievement. His other postwar novels, narrated in the present but largely enacted in the recent past of the 1920s and 1930s, are less successful. There are two mainly political novels: *Lägg undan solen* (*Put Away the Sun,* 1951) and *Favel ensam* (*Favel Alone*, 1968); and a highly ambitious retelling of his own Continental experiences of the 1920s, a kind of continuation of *The Novel About Olof: Romantisk berättelse* (*Romantic Tale*, 1953) and *Tidens gång* (*The Course of Time*, 1955). These books are of considerable interest to literary scholars—they include extracts from Johnson's letters from the Continent to Rudolf Värnlund in Stockholm—but they have not aroused much enthusiasm among the reading public.

Although Johnson is most important as a novelist, he has experimented with other forms of literature. In his youth, as Eyvind Ung, he wrote rousing poems for *Brand*, and he has written occasional poems since then. He has also dramatized some of his novels, mostly for radio; *The Swell on the Beaches* has been given a stage performance and the text published (1948).[36] Translating is another of his activities; in particular, he has translated Sartre and Camus, who seem to have had some influence on his own work. Apart from literature, he has continued to take an active interest in politics since the war, always supporting the claims of democracy and self-determination against the attacks of totalitarian or colonizing powers, whether it be in Hungary or Vietnam. His novels also reveal a highly committed author, though paradoxically—but in the name of freedom—Johnson has defended the author's right to be uncommitted, to be "a little songbird."[37]

Eyvind Johnson has come to be recognized as a leading figure on the Swedish literary scene, a recognition expressed by an honorary doctorate (University of Gothenburg, 1953), by election to the Swedish Academy (the body that awards the Nobel Prize for Literature), and by the Nordic Council's Literature Prize in 1962 for *The Days of His Grace*. Recognition has, however, mostly come from literary and academic circles, for Johnson has acquired nothing like the popularity of, for instance, another distinguished author of his generation, Vilhelm Moberg. His works can seem obscure and ambiguous: his highly developed irony makes no concessions to the casual reader. His roots are deep in the Swedish people—and his autobiographical novel about his youth is easily his most popular work—but he is also, by education, a European intellectual. Norrbotten and Paris: it is a surprising but exceptionally powerful combination.

CHAPTER 2

Experiments

I *The Outsiders*

ONE of the more absorbing aspects of literary research is the study of an author's attempts to come to terms with himself and his art. The financially secure and technically experienced author of later years may turn out perfect works of literature, but there can be something mechanical and predictable about their style and content: the sense of struggle with a recalcitrant material is missing. Yet as a young man the author may have had to fight against reluctant publishers, personal calamities, moments of doubt, poverty, and despair. Something of the sort applies to Eyvind Johnson. He is now a respected member of the Swedish Academy, a writer who can give the slightest article a neat and instantly recognizable turn of phrase, while his early efforts reveal the stresses of a young writer struggling hard for spiritual balance, and at the same time feeling his way through different forms of the novel. Johnson himself exploits the contrast with typical self-irony in his autobiographical novel *Romantic Tale,* where the older author retells the story of the younger.

The main characters in Johnson's early books find themselves somehow outside society, not because they necessarily deliberately dissociate themselves from other men, but because they happen to be different. They have little will of their own; they drift, with only occasional attempts to change direction. The author himself comes to characterize them as Hamlet figures, and with much justification. They are often aware that the time is out of joint, but they are as incapable as Hamlet of doing anything about it. Their actions are spasmodic and uncoordinated, results of temporary convictions. Often they come to grief, and if they survive it is only by settling for the second best. All this is exemplified by Johnson's first book, a collection of four short stories called *De fyra främlingarna* (*The Four Strangers,* 1924). The title aptly describes the main characters in the stories, for all discover they are outsiders.

One of them falls foul of society's economic system, in a story called "Moder Hunger" ("Mother Hunger"). As a child he starves; as a man he discovers the alternative is slavery: "This is life. This is its deepest, innermost meaning: work. Money—we are the ones who give it its value. If we didn't work and eat everything would stand idle, silent and lifeless. We work for the sake of our stomachs, and now I am a slave" (29). When he attempts to break out of his slavery by robbing a safe, he is imprisoned; and his sister's efforts to earn a living involve prostitution.

The author's indignation in "Mother Hunger" leads to melodrama. The same is true of "Snickarprofessor Tantalus" ("Joiner-Professor Tantalus"), about a working-class youth who tries to acquire a middle-class education by his own efforts. His striving for knowledge is as hopeless as Tantalus's attempts to satisfy his desires. He is rejected by his fellow workers, mocked by the well-to-do, and finally goes to his death as an outcast. The other two stories in the collection are more restrained. "Lea och våren" ("Lea and Spring") concerns a girl who shares her biblical namesake's ugliness, and as a result her dreams of love are either frustrated or exploited. She is unable to determine her fate: "She realizes that a life like hers is not a matter of Choosing or Renouncing, Wishing or Believing; she realizes that it is only a question of Letting It Happen, an aimless climbing to the heights, an aimless wandering down to the depths . . ." (181). The fourth story is the only one with a relatively happy ending. "Vallberg" is the name of an aging amusement-stall owner in the north of Sweden who is outwitted by a younger rival. His fellow citizens laugh at his humiliation, and he discovers suddenly that he is a stranger among them. But he then realizes that this is his salvation. He refuses to be bothered by his mockers, goes his own way, and regains some sort of personal integrity, at the price of prosperity. "Vallberg" is the most successful of the four stories and the only one to be republished. Both the subject matter and the half-mocking, half-sympathetic treatment point to Johnson's later works, but for the moment it is the more discordant notes that predominate.

Johnson's first novel, *Timans och rättfärdigheten* (*Timans and Justice,* 1925), concerns an outsider at the other end of the social scale, an over-privileged young man torn between his own background and his sense of solidarity with the under-privileged. Stig Timan is the son of a factory owner. As a child Stig shows signs of maladjustment and hysteria, and in adolescence he revolts against his father's world and sides with the workers: "The adolescent's loneliness is a country that blood and thought long to escape from. It is a tragic fate, oppressive like guilt and gripping the soul like hopeless poverty . . . . His soul wants to create. If he is a worker he gropes for means, instruments, weapons, to take his revenge on loneliness or on others. And if he is not a worker he wants to descend to the damned to liberate himself in their liberation" (36–37). This combination of somewhat melodramatic psychological analysis and highly charged language is typical of the book, and well suited at any rate to the life Stig finds when he comes from Sweden to a Berlin struggling in the aftermath of the World War. He feels tremendous guilt for all the misery he sees, and he is driven to attending workers' meetings and listening to the various solutions speakers propose to the world's economic and social problems. But Stig's cynicism prevents him from playing more than the observer's role: "What was to come? Ridiculous—people prophesied about what was to come. Out of all this old stuff? Everything had something old-fashioned, tortured, monotonous, ridiculous about it. He saw how everything was repeated; century after century, year after year had the same vague mixture of good and evil— . . ." (59–60).

On his return to Sweden Stig finds his best friend Rolf Nyström, one of his father's employees, in the hospital after losing an arm in an accident at the factory. Stig tries to help his friend, but Rolf rejects his charity. The workers have their rights, and one day they will come to claim them. Stig sees that vicarious suffering is useless, and he is even more deeply afflicted with guilt. Rolf, however, undergoes an abrupt religious conversion in the hospital, and his militancy gives way to a sickly humility. When Stig's father hands over the running of the factory to his newly acquired son-in-law, Axel, Rolf becomes Axel's lackey. Axel is the archetypal capitalist. He reduces the workers' wages and provokes a strike, and Rolf supports him throughout. But when the police charge the strikers Rolf suffers an equally abrupt reconversion, goes to his comrades' help, and is shot by the police. The book comes to an end with Stig's sister dying in childbirth, revealing that she has really been in love with Rolf the whole time; with Stig's father collapsing into senility; and with Stig himself as irresolute as ever.

Johnson seems to attempt too much in *Timans and Justice*; he subordinates the plot and the characters to the goal of making as obvious as possible as many ideas as possible. The effects of social division are sufficiently clear without the last-minute revelation about Rolf and Stig's sister; and Rolf's conversion is dictated more by the author's desire to attack religious movements than by anything else. There is, too, in the background the suggestion of inherited guilt, the handing down of the sins of the fathers, that scarcely suits an otherwise starkly realistic novel. Yet the hectic quality of the language conveys an exuberance that saves the book; and perhaps what finally survives is the study of poor, indecisive Stig Timan, aware of what should be done, but unable to do it. Like the outsiders in *The Four Strangers* he drifts, as he explains when Rolf asks him:

> "What path are you following, and where does it lead?"
> Stig Timan looked at him, surprised.
> "What path? My own."
> "Where does it lead then?" Nyström said even more sharply, as if he suddenly felt superior.
> "I really don't know," Stig said jokingly. And more seriously: "How should I know—." (141)

Stad i mörker (*Town in Darkness*, 1927) is a novel of quite a different kind. While *Timans and Justice* is largely constructed out of short scenes, *Town in Darkness* is told in a smaller number of more developed episodes, and the language is more measured. The story is set in a small Swedish town shivering under the northern lights of an arctic winter. In the endless winter night the inhabitants are forced in on themselves and on one another: the young dissipate their energies in drink, while their mothers gossip over their coffee cups and their fathers slip surreptitiously after Venus, town prostitute and sole pedestrian on the deserted streets. Against the emptiness and cold, two characters, Hammar and Andersson, act out a strange rivalry. Hammar, a watchmaker, has worked his way up from a humble apprenticeship to a secure financial and social position. He now feels ready to set the seal on his career by becoming a town councillor: "I don't want to go round like an old man and point with my stick and say that things ought to be different or that they're all wrong. No, I want to be involved and change things. I don't want to be an old man when I'm not"

(235–36). Andersson, a schoolteacher, adopts a totally negative attitude to the town and its councillors. He feels that the community, or rather his fear of its opinions, has ruined his life. As his family's hope, a promising student and graduate, he was more or less forced into becoming a schoolteacher, when his real desire was to be a seaman—for that would have been socially unacceptable. At the start of the novel Hammar and Andersson are at a civic banquet, and Hammar makes his opening bid for a seat on the council with a speech. It is well received, and Hammar is elated, until he sees Andersson looking at him with a cynical smile. He is uneasy, wondering if the schoolteacher is a potential rival, or if he mocks his aspirations. The truth lies in between. Andersson does indeed reject the parliamentary ideal of the town council and its petty-bourgeois values; but he is also worried by Hammar: "One day the watchmaker could surprise him with something he'd thought up on his own. The schoolteacher dreaded that day. It would prove to him that he had lost something, had suffered a defeat, made a mistake, and had been left behind, passed by, had aged. He wanted to be *ahead* of all the others, and to show this he had suspended a cruel smile at the side of his mouth" (164). Certainly Hammar and the other citizens see Andersson's smile as a sign of superiority; but the author reveals it hides "frustration, hopelessness, poverty" (57).

At first Hammar is seen through Andersson's eyes, as a political opportunist without ability or ideals. But the point of view subtly changes. Hammar grows in stature, for he is naively unaware of the means he uses in his climb to power, and he does have a genuine feeling for the town. The unspoken conflict between Hammar and Andersson reaches a climax when Hammar sees a vision of the community as one big family, while Andersson is driven to the other extreme, the ideal of an anarchic life at sea: "Our boat drives blindly, we do not steer it" (248). He rejects the town and its way of life: "I won't love your town. Go away from me! I don't want to love anything; there is nothing to love, and I see too clearly. I don't want to be satisfied, do you hear, I want to perform something extraordinary, something astounding, and I want to do it alone" (238). In desperation he decides to run away to sea.

Then two events completely upset the balance. Hammar's son is drowned after a drunken brawl and, almost accidentally, Andersson seduces the school cleaning woman. Hammar suddenly finds his sense of purpose destroyed, and he asks the schoolteacher for help. Andersson replies that all he can offer is his friendship, and he cries out bitterly: "Hammar, my friend, if I believed in God I should ask him to save us from our thoughts!" (285). Life is cruel and hostile, like the northern winter, but thinking about it makes it doubly so. Andersson sees that his defense against life's disappointments has become a prison. He proceeds to propose to the cleaner, and he sums up his new philosophy:

> We do not need to believe much, for there is so little to believe, but we shouldn't grimace. Not among the crowd, not in solitude. If we grimace we ultimately become petrified, and feel we are petrifying, and want to escape, want to get away, want to live, and we imagine we can do it better and more happily and freely somewhere else. We want to get away and don't know, don't realize that the grimace will accompany us. We don't realize that the only journey that can save us is that from the brain to the heart . . . [And] when we travel to our hearts we should take our brains with us . . . . We should think about those who can't smile. We should curse the world because it's evil and unjust to so many, but we should smile at spring when it comes and talk words of the future. (288–89)

In *Town in Darkness* the outsider comes to terms with himself and with society. This sense of harmony is felt too in the pace of the story, which is more leisurely than in *Timans and Justice*. Johnson demonstrates here his stylistic range and skill: his irony (such as calling the civic banquet "Symposion"); his exuberant and biting sarcasm; and on the other hand his sympathetic and lyrical account of the postmistress's disappointed love. Yet Johnson must have found this more controlled form insufficient for his needs, for in his following works he breaks up the ordered patterns and reestablishes chaos.

Stad i ljus (*Town in Light*, 1928) is necessarily somewhat shapeless because of its subject. The scene is Paris on July 14, and the festive city is experienced through a young Swedish writer, Torsten, who wanders destitute and starving through the crowds, thinking about the registered letter and the money from Sweden that can save him. He soaks up sensations, tries to suppress the pangs of hunger with a kind of black humor, attempts to borrow money, but refuses it when it is offered. Like his predecessors in Johnson's stories he stands outside society, and like them he too seems incapable of controlling his own fate. The only guiding line in his action is a desire to understand what is happening to him and to

write it down in "The Book": "I want to get through to my century;
that is, I want to know what it's like. Do we know what it's like?
No. And I want to get through to myself. I want to know why I
write, why I'm living to write, why I'm waiting for something
and what I'm waiting for. . . . *I want to know who I am!*" (115).
The novel is told in the form of a letter, written by a friend of
Torsten's. The author follows Torsten's progress through the
city and to some extent allows his character to determine the composition: "Torsten walked as he has walked throughout this
book. He continued without regard to style or composition . . ."
(128). But the author does not consistently follow Torsten's point
of view. For example, he breaks off to give a resumé of Torsten's
life in Stockholm before his arrival in Paris, and now and then
he bursts into prose poems, such as "The Town's Song at Dinner
Time" (60–61). The book leaves a rather blurred impression,
for the focus of attention seems sometimes to be Torsten, sometimes Paris, and the connection between the two is really fortuitous.

Divided attention is also an obvious reaction to Johnson's next
novel, *Minnas* (*Remembering,* 1928), which tends to split into
two stories. The scene is once more a town in the north of Sweden,
where the librarian, Doctor Clerk, watches over the inhabitants
"calmly and sorrowfully like a father with many different and
unreliable children" (146). His protective, and to some extent
unifying, eye rests on a widowed mother, Antonia Berr, and her
two sons, Ivar and Martin; and also on an ex-Guardsman, J. A.
Galén. Yet there is little Clerk can do to arrest the calamitous
events in this anguished novel. Mrs. Berr is run over by a truck;
Ivar Berr falls in love with a faithless girl and sinks deeper and
deeper into despair and alcoholism; Martin Berr studies hard
as a promising scholar, only to be strangled by Galén, who mo-
mentarily succumbs to latent homosexual impulses. It is understandable that Mr. Clerk dare not open his mouth at Martin's
funeral: "He felt as if he had it full of earth, which he had to swallow
so as not to spit it out as bitter hate of the powers that rule in men's
breasts and guide men's fates" (288). It is these powers, rather
than their effects, that are the author's preoccupation. The conflict between man and society that is so important in *Timans and
Justice* and *Town in Darkness* is subordinated to the conflicts
within the individual that cause him to cut himself off from his
fellow human beings.

Firstly there is Clerk. He is distant and reserved, sympathetic but scarcely friendly. In his youth he had an affair with Mrs. Berr, and Ivar is his son. Mrs. Berr, however, decided to marry someone else, and Clerk has tried to overcome his distress by simply forgetting it all, by living with "the dead memories" (58): "Mr. Clerk wanted memories to be old clothes he had taken off—nothing more; old clothes you hang up in the wardrobe but never wear again" (60). However, one of the points the novel makes is that memories cannot be treated so easily. One day Clerk discovers an old letter from Mrs. Berr, and his memories immediately overwhelm him; he cannot control them after all. A further reminder is that he sees his past repeated in the life of his son, Ivar Berr. Mrs. Berr's sons represent different sides of Clerk. Martin is the intellectual, while Ivar is "my worse, my other being, who walks the streets because of a bit of paper" (168). Ivar pursues a woman called Birgit, but she passes from man to man as her body dictates. She grows tired of Ivar, but does not break altogether with him, and for him the parting is a long-drawn-out agony. His pursuit of Birgit occupies all his time and separates him from his mother and brother; even when his mother lies dying he is hanging hopefully round Birgit's door. Clerk tries on several occasions to talk with Ivar about his problems, but Ivar rejects his help: the friendship that held men together in *Town in Darkness* is no longer sufficient. Ivar escapes from his memories of Birgit by drinking; and when his brother is murdered he has to escape altogether from the town: "Ivar Berr had made his decision to leave, and the decision was like that a man makes when he meets a car at a bend. He jumps out of the way and does not consider if it is to the right or left. He quite simply jumps to one side so as not to be run over" (291).

A third character in the book who tries hard to cope with his memories is Galén. He is homosexual by nature, and his career in the army has involved some incident with a drummer boy, but he tries to suppress both his memories and his inclinations. While Clerk copes with his memories by freezing his emotional life, Galén tries to disguise his impulses by thinking of them as temptations of demons, temptations which can only be met by drinking bouts. Galén's problems are aggravated by a malicious old pauper called Zeitz, who tells him that a previous occupant of the Galéns' house murdered his wife and then committed suicide. Sickened by his wife's sexual demands, Galén becomes obsessed with the idea of history's repeating itself. Clerk is aware of Galén's problems as he is of Ivar's, but again he cannot help. In a weak moment Galén makes advances to Martin Berr, who recoils from them. In Galén's confused mind Zeitz, Martin, and the past merge, and in an effort to rid himself of his demons Galén strangles Martin.

Remembering is a significant novel in Johnson's development. The importance of memories in his works can scarcely be exaggerated; it is equally great in a novel like *The Days of His Grace*, written over thirty years later. Important too is the subject of despair and man's fight against it, and his attempts to achieve balance. However, the novel is not a complete success. The two separate stories of Galén and Ivar Berr are not sufficiently interwoven for them to be counted as one story. The psychological analysis can seem more literary than penetrating, and the author sabotages more serious interpretations by caricaturing his characters. Their names cast them as types rather than individuals: *clerk* means "scholar," *galen* means "mad," while *Zeitz*, whose family is of German origin, suggests the German word *Zeit*, "time," which apparently introduces a touch of symbolism into Galén's murdering.

In *Commentary on a Falling Star* Johnson makes a more impressive attempt at similar themes. The novel is woven out of several plots, and the result is a cross-section of life in Stockholm in the late 1920s. One plot centers around Carl-Alfred Stormdal, an importer of oranges. He is a self-made man, the son of a joiner, who has achieved financial success and thus social respectability. He has married a penniless but aristocratic wife, Laura, and he has just set the seal on his success with the Knight's Cross of the Order of Vasa, awarded him for a donation to an orphanage. Now, however, his concentration relaxes, and his apparently stable mind is rapidly unbalanced by a combination of accident and design. The novel begins with a walk he takes through Stockholm, and on this walk he passes a banana peel, thrown down on the road. He does not consciously notice this peel, but gradually he becomes more and more aware of discarded banana peels, and he is worried—ostensibly by the danger to people's safety, but subconsciously too by the threat to his trade in oranges. His preoccupation becomes a minor obsession, and is somehow associated with the Order of Vasa. Laura is uneasy and calls in a psychiatrist, who starts from the assumption that Stormdal must be mad and soon causes his assumption to become true. Laura also begins to change. She has no affection for her husband and despises his working-class habits, and when the suggestion is made that Stormdal may be declared incapable of managing his own affairs, she begins to see the advantage of having her husband out of the way. Stormdal is sent to a mental hospital and goes completely to pieces. He finds himself hopelessly adrift, a man who has been successful in business by cutting himself loose from his home background, by abandoning his mistresses, and by marrying without love. He has attempted to suppress his natural gestures and language and imitate his wife's style of living; as the author notes: "When Laura was not present he seemed like a proper human being" (37). Fortunately he is able to make the spiritual journey back to his beginnings, and he is helped by the one genuine emotion in his superficial life—his love of nature, particularly oak trees. He escapes from hospital and comes back to confront Laura, but he is a broken man and no match for her. Instead he goes out once more on a walk through Stockholm, now in the middle of winter. Leaning against an oak tree in a park, he thinks back, until he returns to his childhood: "Stormdal closed his eyes and time rolled further and further back. He was standing on a hill somewhere in southern Stockholm one windy winter's day and holding his mother's hand. A small boy waiting for his father one Saturday afternoon. Johansson the carpenter comes up the hill, bearing the day's labors like a burden. There is a smell of sweat, healthy sweat, about him, a smell of wood, paint, and plaster" (301). At peace with himself at last, Stormdal curls up under the tree and freezes to death.

Stormdal's marriage is childless, but he has two sons by different mistresses. The elder of the half-brothers is Magnus Lyck, the younger is Andreas Sonath. Magnus's mother has proved too humble for Stormdal, and although he has made generous financial provision for her and Magnus, she regards his marriage to Laura as a betrayal. She takes Magnus out to the island of Kråkön in Lake Mälaren, near Stockholm, and tells him: "You must never forget this, Magnus: that your mother sat like a wretch on an island in Mälaren when your father got married one midsummer eve. Remember as well that we need water and grass and trees round us sometimes. When you're older you'll understand" (20). Magnus rejects his father's world, seizes on his own proletarian background, and joins the Communists. But he becomes infatuated with a promiscuous young actress, Eva, and his revolutionary zeal is undermined by his personal problems. He also finds himself abandoned on Kråkön, for when he comes to the island with Eva to celebrate midsummer he finds she is more interested in his half-brother. Magnus speaks defiantly to the island: "To be or not to be, that is not the question. We can live without illusions; many do. Illusions—we treat them like this: we watch them tumble down .... I'm one of those who have a philosophy, I place myself above private affairs and don't go around bothering about my soul or my heart. Love sits in the testicles, in the ovaries—that is the clear vision that will save the world. I'm no wretch, no Hamlet" (34). In practice, however, he is as much a Hamlet as his predecessors in Johnson's novels, and he becomes as passive a spectator of his fate as they are. He becomes "*the eye,* the powerless eye that followed everything but could not intervene" (67). Like his father and mother he has to find his consolation in nature, and at the end of the novel he again sits on Kråkön, on May 1, as his former comrades carry their banners through the capital. He lights a fire and communes with it:

Illusions—we tear them down like this. And we build them up again, like this. For we need them, they're what we find when we look for Paradise but tumble into Hell, and it's better for us to find them than for the world to be empty. We ask our way forwards. We solve old problems with new questions. We take heaven to pieces to get at the truth. We dig down into the earth with our questions, deeper and deeper. And it's lucky we can ask, that we can make grand gestures and hurl our question marks at the vault above us. Perhaps all progress depends on a new, a more intelligent, a more ingenious way of asking .... There is hope in every question, and a man who hopes looks to the future.   (312)

Magnus seems to accept that his role must be that of a Hamlet. He cannot adopt a faith unquestioningly, believing where he cannot prove. When he thinks of the marching crowds, he declares that he is faithful to them in his fashion, but his fashion is more critical and passive. Yet Hamlet's role is important: by asking questions, by searching for truth, he makes his own valuable contribution to human progress. Magnus's speech to the fire marks the culmination of a period of restless—sometimes agonized—introspection in Johnson's novels and leads on, through *Farewell to Hamlet,* to the more harmonious, outward-looking probings of the Mårten Torpare novels.

The other characters in *Commentary on a Falling Star* scarcely arouse the same interest as Stormdal and Magnus, or the same sympathy. Laura consoles herself for her husband's absence by having an affair with his younger son, Andreas. Andreas, a violinist, specializes in living off rich widows and comes to Laura after leaving a less well-off widow with the consolation of a child. Stormdal's brother Nils, who spends all day in the Royal Library working on a gigantic history of the world, acts with a similar lack of emotion. Yet the author clearly wants to show that people are not wholly good or wholly evil. They are not set in a particular mould; rather they are battlegrounds for conflicting, often subconscious, interests and emotions. Laura's infidelity is presented in the following terms: "Laura may not have been cruel, but she had the ability to ignore, to avoid thinking about certain things and to avoid wanting things, when this wanting might involve the least bit of unpleasantness for her . . . . No, Laura was not cruel. It was merely the weight of forty-five years pressing on her that she wanted to throw off" (151). Nils and Andreas, usually so cold and self-absorbed, can show signs of decency. Andreas dives into Mälaren to rescue a would-be suicide. Nils, who subsists on grants from his brother, is refused help by Laura and goes off to complain to his brother in the mental hospital and tell him about Laura's infidelity. Yet he finds he cannot, even though it means he will be forced to earn his own living for the first time.

The various stories in *Commentary on a Falling Star* are more closely connected than the two plots of *Remembering*. In the first place the characters are connected by blood or friendship, and their paths cross frequently. More important, though, their lives all illustrate one underlying idea in the novel—the bankruptcy of bourgeois society and its capitalist and cultural values. Stormdal has ceased to be true to himself by chasing after money, and his story is paralleled by that of Emil Larsson, a comrade of Magnus's, who makes a fortune but loses his soul. Laura's breeding hides a sterility of emotion, as does Nils's academic manner. The two artists—Eva the actress and Andreas the violinist—are similarly superficial. The characters have cut themselves off from the basic sources of strength: their childhood memories and the regenerative powers of nature. Stormdal finds his way back to his childhood home; Magnus searches desperately for a father, or even a grandfather; but Nils shows not the slightest interest in his ancestry. The parallels and contrasts

are all well drawn, but naturally the theme of sterility and super-
ficiality makes depressing reading.

II   *Influences and Techniques*

Searching in one author's works for influences from another's
is always a risky business, and especially so in the case of an author
like Eyvind Johnson. He is widely read, scattering authors' names
through his articles and diaries in daunting numbers. He has stated
quite openly that literature is an important source of material for
him: the novelist's personal impressions are necessarily limited,
and he must make use of other people's, through the medium of
literature.[1]

Of possible influences, Örjan Lindberger writes as follows:
"It would be a long list, beginning with German Expressionism
and Hamsun, continuing with French Surrealism, then with
Bergson and Proust, Gide and Joyce, containing, too, examples
of breadthwise cutting such as Dos Passos's *The 42d Parallel* or
Döblin's *Berlin Alexanderplatz*, the lessons of Thomas Mann
and Hesse, and more recently a debate with Existentialism. Behind
all this we should now and then catch a glimpse of the shadow
of Henry James."[2] Of these authors Johnson himself has emphasized
the importance of Proust, Gide, and Joyce, and a consideration
of these three novelists throws light on Johnson's development
up to *Commentary on a Falling Star*.

In 1931 Johnson published three articles on the novel, in the
magazine *Fronten (The Front)*. The first is an enthusiastic account
of developments in the novel in Europe and America, the second
is an attack on the corresponding backwardness of the Swedish
novel, and the third article discusses some Swedish novelists who
are honorable exceptions to the general state of reaction.[3] Johnson
later republished the arguments of the first article, expanding and
amplifying them, in *Avsikter (Intentions, 1945)*.[4] Johnson sees
the author's task as being that of a mediator. He must give life to
abstract ideas and convey them through his writings to a larger
audience. He must open people's eyes as to what is happening
round them: "[Literature's] most important task is to interpret
the present to the people of the present" (*Fronten*, No. 2). There
is an obvious consequence to this: "The forms of existence change.
Consequently, a form of writing that is particularly aimed at de-

scribing the changes and moods of human existence and reproducing its psychology must do likewise, or it becomes untrue. The novelist is the servant of life" (*Fronten*, No. 2). It is not so much life itself or basic human emotions that change, but our way of looking at them. In an earlier article, from 1926, Johnson had claimed that Freud and Bergson have completely altered man's way of seeing himself. Previously human beings were considered to be reasonably homogeneous, but now it seems "a man can have several faces and his 'soul' is a conglomeration of a thousand whims and a thousand states of mind," and he is in a constant process of change: "No one can tell the whole truth about himself or others—'I am like this, you are like that.' No one can say what he or she is *really* like."[5]

The novel must come to terms with the new psychology, and Johnson finds the most suitable techniques in Proust, Gide, and Joyce. He praises them for introducing "new ways of observing man and his circumstances, new ways of describing the acquired experiences. Each of them has in his own way opened the eyes of others to new or latent possibilities in the novel" (*Intentions*, 82). Joyce is synonymous with *Ulysses,* of which Johnson writes: "Joyce's intention is plain: to try to give as exhaustive a description as possible of a human life, of human life" (83). As for Proust, Johnson praises his method of "the minutest reproduction of external events and psychical reactions, and careful investigations of the contents of memory" (84). Gide is first and foremost the author of *The Counterfeiters:* "It is noble French Classicism in conjunction with a new knowledge of man, a modern understanding and a ruthless analysis of human beings, with modulations of voice, elements of mysticism and a striving towards the ultimate limits of thinking, and an alternately calm, alternately trembling, not judgment, but observation of the phenomenon of man" (85). Amplification of these remarks about Gide is to be found in three articles Johnson wrote in 1927.[6] In the first of these he again praises Gide's "passion for thought" and notes: "There is a grand *idea,* which as the work progresses develops, clarifies, assumes solid shape, and finally, together with the major and minor events in the work, is terminated, rounded off, and lies ready and complete on the last page." And in a review of a Swedish translation of *The Counterfeiters* from 1932 Johnson talks of the novel as "one of the strangest constructions of modern literature. It begins one

day—no day in particular—and ends another day—no day in
particular—and captures a slice of life's endless confusion of
shapes and thoughts, a glimpse of the restlessness of our times, both
in society and the individual. And it has no real ending."[7]

What, then, did Johnson learn from these three innovators?
First, Proust. According to Lindberger, Johnson came to Proust
indirectly in 1925—through a book about him and his work—and
started reading *Remembrance of Things Past* in the fall of 1926.[8]
There is a reference to Proust in *Town in Light,* which was finished
about this time. There Torsten thinks: "If one had time one could
write such articles, write about one thing at a time, look carefully
at every street to find something special about it, discover, enjoy
discovering, write one word, one line after another, read through
it, supplement it, write long parentheses like Marcel Proust, parentheses within parentheses, be careful, be wise, shape things" (90).
Johnson seems to make two points about Proust: his exhaustive
descriptions, and his involved style. He makes no further attempt
in *Town in Light* or the immediately following novels to imitate
this, and by the time his own style has become scarcely less intricate
and exhaustive than Proust's, it is not possible to say with any
certainty that Proust is the major cause. Rather, it seems to be
Proust's "careful investigations of the contents of memory" that
immediately appealed to Johnson. Lindberger notes Johnson's
first attempts to exploit a complicated interplay of different periods
of time in a man's consciousness in a short story, "Brev till en dam"
("Letter to a Lady," 1927).[9] Johnson did not, of course, need Proust
to tell him of the importance of memory, but the illustrations and
discussions of the *processes* of remembering that appear in Johnson's
novels, beginning with *Remembering,* may possibly be prompted
by Proust (and Bergson). *Remembering* contains little Proustian
touches, scenes that seem to copy the opening scene of *Remembrance
of Things Past.* One example of this is when Ivar Berr lies between
sleep and waking: "He tried to sleep. Confused and changed the
images of the day rose up in his half-slumber" (15). Involuntary
memory—memory developed out of a kind of trance, or memory
suddenly sparked off by some external event—becomes a theme
of the greatest importance in Johnson's work. His subject matter
may be very different from Proust's, but his methods of introducing
memories into his novels seem to owe something to *Remembrance
of Things Past.*

Next, Gide. In his articles Johnson distinguishes two qualities he admires in Gide: his passionate and persistent pursuit of ideas, and his comprehensive view of life—"breadthwise cutting." "Breadthwise cutting" is a phrase taken from *The Counterfeiters;* it is used by the writer Edouard in the chapter in which he develops his ideas of the novel (Part II, Ch. 3): "'A slice of life,' the Naturalist school said. The great mistake of that school is that it always cuts its slice in the same direction—in the direction of time, lengthwise. Why not breadthwise? Or depthwise? As for me, I should like not to cut at all. You understand: I should like to get everything into this novel."[10] Instead of pursuing one event over a long period of time, the author can take a cross-section, a breadthwise cutting of life at one moment of time, revealing lots of parallel events, or he can study one person or event in depth at one moment of time; or, of course, he can refuse to be selective and try to get everything into his novel. This enormous challenge was one that Johnson tried to meet later, in *Krilon;* for the moment the most important lesson Gide had to teach him seems to have been breadthwise cutting. *The Counterfeiters* showed him in particular how breadthwise cutting could be exploited in the novel of ideas, for the different stories that make up the novel all illustrate some aspect of the idea of forgery and deception. Johnson clearly attempts something of the sort in *Commentary on a Falling Star,* where he follows several threads simultaneously, and where the separate stories are united by, and illustrate from different angles, one central idea. After *Commentary on a Falling Star* breadthwise cutting becomes a regular feature of Johnson's works, though he never goes so far as to dispense with a definite beginning and end—cutting as it were at random. Gide's influence is obvious on the technical side, but one curious theme—Galén's pederasty—may owe something to him. Certainly, it is a subject otherwise absent in Johnson's works, even when the subject matter is taken from Ancient Greece.

Finally, Joyce. As with Proust, Johnson discovered Joyce at second hand. In the spring of 1928 he met in Paris an American scholar, Joseph Warren Beach. Beach, who was interested in new techniques in the novel, had read *Town in Light* in French translation and been interested by what he saw as its modern construction—perhaps its limitations in time and space. In fact Beach had more to tell Johnson than Johnson had Beach. The meeting is described by Johnson in *The Course of Time* (294–95), and, as remembered

thirty years later, in *Traces past Colonos* (58–60), and by Lindberger,[11] while something of what Beach had to say may be in-
ferred from his book *The Twentieth Century Novel*.[12] Beach must
have discussed Gide's breadthwise cutting and may have given
Johnson an even more extreme example than *The Counterfeiters*,
in James Joyce's *Ulysses*. One section of the novel describes the
activities of a great number of Dubliners at one moment of time,
and some of these Dubliners are related by their common experience
of a viceregal cavalcade.[13] Johnson uses a similar device in his
Torpare novels: in *Bobinack* a car accident, and in *Night Maneuvers* a funeral procession. But *Ulysses* was to provide Johnson
with a much more important idea: "stream of consciousness."
This it was that enabled Joyce to give "as exhaustive a description
as possible" of human beings and the functioning of their minds.
Johnson's first attempt at imitating Joyce's technique—even though
he had not read *Ulysses*—seems to be the short story "Svår stund"
("Difficult Hour," 1928).[14] It is the reproduction, in dialect, of the
thoughts passing through the mind of a railroad worker who is
on the point of hanging himself after disappointment in love.
Johnson began reading *Ulysses* in March, 1929, while he was
working on *Commentary on a Falling Star,* and then he read it in
English, a language he did not know at all well. He seems nonetheless to imitate some of Joyce's traits in Stormdal's monologues,
for example playing on words—particularly by rhyming—and
using literary references and quotations. He makes no attempt,
though, to copy Joyce's poetic and often original language, and
he never lets his monologues become as obscure as those in *Ulysses*
—the trains of thought and associations of ideas are always obvious.[15] Stream of consciousness is similarly used in Johnson's
later works, never being allowed to dominate the presentation or
bewilder the reader. Rather, Johnson uses the technique to give
an immediate and often very effective impression of a character's
range of expression or way of thinking, such as Sander in *The
Soldier's Return,*[16] or Warnefrit Lupigis in a state of impotent and
illiterate rage in *The Days of His Grace* (Ch. 16).

The result of Johnson's acquaintance with Proust, Gide, and
Joyce was that at the beginning of the 1920s he was better equipped
technically than he was imaginatively. His great problem always
seems to have been finding stories sufficiently interesting to carry
the burden of ideas they generally have to bear. When he has taken

his stories from outside his imagination, either from his own life—as in *The Novel About Olof*—or from history, or even from other literature, then his technical skill has supported rather than dwarfed the plot, and he has created novels that are of international standing.

CHAPTER 3

Problems under Debate

I Farewell to Hamlet

IN the 1930s Johnson published five novels with one character in common, Mårten Torpare. These books are devoted to debating contemporary problems, and Mårten acts very much as the author's mouthpiece within the story. As he says in the last of the series, *The Soldier's Return:* "I have passed through several books where I have almost been the main character, but a main character standing beside the author, seeing what he sees, and trying to look with his eyes" (200).

Mårten is undoubtedly the main character in *Avsked till Hamlet* (*Farewell to Hamlet,* 1930), which is the story of his youth. The novel is in four parts. In the first part a childless couple, the parvenu Bombasius and his religious wife, decide to adopt one of their poorer relatives' children. They choose Mårten Torpare, son of a railroad worker and twin brother to a girl called Sigrid, and they bring him up with the intention of making a clergyman of him. He goes to university in Uppsala, but rebels and leaves. Sigrid, meanwhile, has conceived an illegitimate child and has run away from home to join a cabaret act. The twins meet in Copenhagen, then Sigrid dies in childbirth, and Mårten leaves for Paris. In the second part of the novel Mårten moves in a group of impoverished Swedes in Paris, including a resourceful commercial traveler called Merkurius, but he parts from them to live with a French girl—known only as "Mademoiselle." She becomes pregnant, and he decides to marry her, but he loses her, as he had lost Sigrid. She leaves him and has the child aborted. In the third part Mårten is back in Sweden, staying with a man called Pelle in a cottage in the forests of the north. The story is told by Pelle, who entitles his account "Meeting with Hamlet." Mårten and Pelle go to a lecture on "the new man," and after the lecture Mårten seems to have achieved some clarity in his ideas. The result of his meditations is that he returns home, and the fourth part of the novel is concerned with his family. Merkurius suddenly appears, now rich and prosperous, and seduces Mårten's younger sister, Tora. He offers Mårten a job on the tacit understanding that he should acquire Tora as his mistress, but Mårten throws him out. Instead Mårten takes up manual labor. Yet another danger threatens Tora, an evangelist called Ros, who takes her in with his preaching until Mårten punctures his sermons. Mårten is clearly no longer a passive Hamlet. He is a man who can make decisions and act to change the course of events.

Farewell to Hamlet is basically the story of a boy taken from his natural environment, bewildered by his transplanting, and in his bewilderment seeking some faith to live by. He finally finds this faith when he returns to his original surroundings. The theme is therefore a repeat of that of *Commentary on a Falling Star*. The contrast for Mårten between his parents' home, where his father is a casual laborer, and the profession for which he is being educated, the ministry, is disastrous. When, as a student, he gets drunk, he defiantly presents himself as a laborer, and his guilt at betraying his own class by becoming a pastor is aggravated by the need to show Bombasius gratitude for giving him a better chance than his brothers and sisters. Mårten sees a glimmer of hope when he reads a newspaper article by a man who also finds his past a burden and announces his intention to start afresh. Mårten is inspired to follow his example and travels to Denmark as "an interpreter of Hamlet . . . a great interpreter of modern life" (92). However, all his plans are upset by Sigrid's death: "Everything lost its meaning for me when she died; we belonged together, and it was so terrible being alone" (241). It is not only the fact that they are twins. It is that they are opposite and therefore complementary in character. Mårten is reserved and bookish, while Sigrid has rushed headlong into life: "She had lived intensely, her face suddenly became old," Mårten notices at her deathbed (98). He contrasts his reluctant attempts to become a minister with Sigrid's running away to be the actress she really wanted to be: "Sigrid must have meant that we ought to follow our innermost desires to be happy" (128). Sigrid is impulsive, Mårten meditative, two twins who are cruelly separated. And Mårten feels responsible for this separation. When Bombasius had come to adopt a child, Mårten had been pushing Sigrid along in a wheelbarrow, but he had tipped her out and left her to make her own way home. Mårten gives this incident a wider interpretation: "There was a little lad walking down a country road pushing a barrow towards his fate, and that fate was called Bombasius. And my sister was sitting in the barrow and—and—and then I tipped her out, left the cart and carried on all the same—" (177).

Mårten feels that if he had stayed with Sigrid he might have saved her from her hectic and tawdry career. He tries to atone by looking after "Mademoiselle," calling her "little sister on the boulevards" (121), or "little sister Ophelia" (162), but he is no more successful. She returns to the procurer she works for and lives with, and Mårten makes no attempt to intervene. It is not until the situation arises for the third time, in connection with his younger sister Tora, that he is able to act, lying and destroying people's illusions to save her from revivalism. It is not until then that he finally bids farewell to Hamlet. He gains the strength for this from his renewed contact with his proletarian background, with its firm principles and steadfast will: "Civilization . . . is ennobled nature, the discipline of instincts, the will to justice, knowledge of justice. The most important element in civilization at the moment is the workers' movement, because it has the will without which everything is dead. It may not produce the greatest, the finest souls, but it keeps their work alive . . . . A socialist group, a workers' commune, a communist cell, a trade union, a teetotalers' lodge, a cooperative shop is, like a university, a center of civilization" (188–89).

The author of the article that prompts Mårten's journey to Denmark believes in starting afresh, without a past. But when Mårten meets the author—who is in fact Ros—in Paris, he finds him spiritually bankrupt; and when Ros returns to Sweden and becomes an evangelist, Mårten says: "He was very, very much more unhappy than any other person. He had lost himself, he had left himself, without a trace" (152). Mårten himself ultimately comes to realize that he can only begin as a new man not by cutting himself off from his past, but by returning to it and drawing strength from its traditions.

II   The New Society

Farewell to Hamlet is centered on one character, while Johnson's following novel, *Bobinack* (1932), is a more involved account of a number of characters during one week in Stockholm. There is

Kyndel Romaticus, director of a cosmetics firm called Aromatica; his lively, perpetually inquisitive wife Martina; the title character Bobinack and his henchman John Mount; Mårten Torpare, his friend Eleonora, and her former brother-in-law Cederquist; and a girl called Lydia. In just one week their interrelationships completely change their lives. Romaticus has a birthday party, drifts apart from Martina, and ends up living with Lydia; Martina pursues Mount, who shoots Bobinack when he insults her; Cederquist throws himself out of a window at Romaticus's party; and Eleonora deserts Mårten.

The story is dominated by Bobinack, though he himself remains a puzzling figure. Mårten gives some definite facts about him: that he is the son of a Stockholm wholesaler and a Danish musician, that he has been imprisoned for embezzlement, that he has then been abroad, and that he is now in Stockholm to sell a machine for electrical massage, called *Solkraft,* "sun power." More important than his personal background is what he stands for, which is complete freedom from all laws and conventions: "My whole life has been a prison, both a real state prison—I was inside for four years, four years for embezzlement which may not have been embezzlement—and the prison of this civilization. While I was in the first prison I escaped from the second. When I was freed a couple of years ago I had really been free for more than three years" (239). Bobinack now stands outside the society he operates in, beyond its concepts of good and evil.

Mårten is the man best placed to observe Bobinack, and it is the observer's role he plays in this novel: "I live like a taut string, I live like a nerve in the body of mankind" (161). He is not so blinkered by the obsessions of the other characters: "I am really on a different wavelength. I belong to those who wander . . . . Behind me lies a collection of documents in which you can find out what it was like where I went" (262). Mårten sees Bobinack as something new in the world, possibly "the new man," possibly merely a confidence trickster, but in any case a man freed from tradition and the past:

He was no person, believe me, he was a spirit. Personally I think he was the Devil, but I have no positive proof . . . . I mean a devil who is Lucifer, Prometheus, and Bodin the tightrope walker, the one who walked above Niagara Falls. And that's something. Bobinack was completely without

regard for anything. He had suffered much and been cast out from the
dwellings of the blessed. He wanted to spread light, give back fire to mankind. He roamed beyond the boundaries drawn round bourgeois society
by judicial and moral laws and ideas. He was very daring and could devote
an enormous amount of energy to actions completely meaningless in the
eyes of ordinary people. He was all that is irrational.   (317–18)

Because Bobinack acts so strangely, Mårten has no idea what his
real aims are. He can only describe the effect Bobinack has on
him, particularly in the overwhelming laugh he laughs before
Mount shoots him: "There was such evil in the laugh that we
felt paralyzed—we couldn't do anything. It convinced me that
Bobinack must be the Devil. But at the same time there was a
great deal of sense and goodness in his laugh. It was connected
with spring, with life, with freedom, or at least longing for freedom" (319).

While Bobinack's actual occupation is selling opiates to the
society he so deeply despises, Mårten does not think his aim is
making money. He merely likes setting things in motion, disturbing
the calm. Something of the sort seems to lie behind Bobinack's
major achievement in the book: the destruction of the order in
Romaticus's life. Romaticus is the son of a caretaker, but he
has made a fortune with his cosmetics firm and uses his money
to keep him well away from his proletarian background. His life,
however, is empty. His marriage to Martina is harmonious but no
more, his business functions automatically, and he spends his
time reading detective novels. He is as easily destroyed as Stormdal
in *Commentary on a Falling Star*.

Bobinack sits talking to Romaticus one night, and appointing
himself "God's representative" (203) he mentions the futility of
Aromatica, and its bad effect on Romaticus's spiritual life. Bobinack
tries to bring Romaticus to God—that is, a more spiritual existence
—via Christ, particularly the agony of the crucifixion, which he
describes in gruesome detail, but Romaticus is too superficial to
feel deeply. Bobinack then changes his role to that of the Devil:

We others suffer or have suffered hell—I, Mount, all the others—why
should you have the right to be happier? You're scarcely worth it. You're
nothing; you're a bubble. You have no faith, no regrets for anything, no
anxiety about the future; there is only satisfaction, stupid satisfaction, in

everything you do. I thought I would represent God a while. But it has no effect on you. What would you say if we were to play hell a little while? You are the victim, you represent bourgeois man, selfish, egoistic, self-satisfied, and I, who am unknown, represent the Devil. (238)

Then Bobinack reveals that Martina has been deeply involved in the past with Mount. Suddenly Romaticus understands what suffering is: he can see Christ limping in front of him. His world is destroyed. He leaves Martina and lives instead with Lydia, who is a complete child of nature, living by her instincts, in dreams of Brazil and uninhibited Negroes.

The contrast between Romaticus and Bobinack is only one illustration of the idea that underlies the various stories in the novel: that capitalist, bourgeois society is in its death throes, and that it must give way to a more spontaneous, primitivist way of life. John Mount and Cederquist are different sides of bourgeois man, Bobinack claims (237). Mount has tried hard to free himself from his social background but failed. He becomes merely a criminal, and a man who cannot break laws and conventions without a sense of shame. Cederquist on the other hand clings to his moral code, and when he becomes drunk and makes a declaration of love to Martina he realizes he cannot live with this breach of good behavior, and he commits suicide. The world he represents is set on a similarly disastrous course. As the equally bourgeois Eleonora cries: "You talk about an old and a new world, but for us there is nothing to hold fast to, we can only go under. They are getting at us. We can't defend ourselves, we don't know what it means to be a new generation and we haven't the strength or the desire to believe in the values of the civilization we are the fruits of" (260).

Mårten Torpare is left to point the moral, but he is far from preaching an extreme doctrine: "After reading and rereading Rousseau, he wrote and wanted to prove that if we return to nature (so as at least to be able to reinvigorate our instincts), we ought to take a radio and toothbrush with us and incorporate them with nature" (57). His attitude is experimental. Like Magnus Lyck in *Commentary on a Falling Star,* he wants to feel his way forward by asking questions. In a closing message to the author Mårten explains: "At the moment I am investigating the value of man's accumulated experiences, culture. I'm not sure that bourgeois culture, the only one at present in stock when you go into a shop and demand a bit of culture, is so vitally important that we should give our lives for it. Are you? Nor am I absolutely convinced that bourgeois society is the only possible form of society" (321).

The construction of *Bobinack* is intricate, yet basically simple. The novel opens with a car crash, at which nearly all the characters are present. The crash is in a way a symbol of the fate of bourgeois society—at any rate Bobinack and Cederquist see it that way. The actual cause of the crash is not explained until three-quarters of the way through the book, but the story begins immediately from it, for the author follows the paths of the characters as they disperse in different directions. It then turns out they all have points of contact with each other, by blood, marriage, or acquaintance: a veritable cat's cradle of interlaced threads. Not only the car crash gathers them together: there is one page representing a page of a newspaper (101), where the different articles all concern the actions of characters in the novel; and a final point of focus is Bobinack's death, at which all are present. One particular feature of *Bobinack*, which is repeated in the later Mårten Torpare novels, is the relationship between this novel and earlier novels. It is a little game Johnson plays with his readers, openly when he lets Martina say to Mårten that "a book has been written about you. Hamlet, Hamlet!" (96), more coyly when he gives Bobinack exactly the same parentage as Andreas Sonath in *Commentary on a Falling Star*.

Regn i gryningen (*Rain at Dawn*, 1933) takes the investigations into a return to nature a little further. The first part of the novel describes a man's attempt to become a respectable middle-class citizen, while the second part describes his efforts to destroy the way of life he has acquired. Henrik Fax is born illegitimate into a peasant family, but he gains some education, moves to town, and becomes an office worker. He works his way up in society until he acquires a wife, Kat, a daughter, Gull, and his own house. Yet he feels he has gone wrong somewhere, or as Kat indignantly remarks: "'Sometimes I think you're not really serious about what you say to me, about what you do, Henrik. Just as if your job, this house, Gull, me, were nothing of real value to you, only something temporary . . . .' He felt that in a way she was right; he protested, but she was right" (40). He goes to a lecture given by Mårten Torpare, who tells his audience they should break up from their old lives, though he will not tell them what they should aim at instead. Henrik Fax decides to take his advice, and he abandons his job and his family and returns to his childhood cottage in the country.

In his rural solitude Fax composes "Henrik Fax's Book about Real Life," which forms the second part of *Rain at Dawn*. It is the account of his search for the truth about his life, combined with his day-to-day experiences in the country and thoughts about life in general. Fax begins his story by recounting the events of his life, which the author has already related more objectively in the first part of the novel. Two women dominate Fax's past: Rosa, with whom he had his first big love affair, and Kat. His affair with Rosa lies twelve years in the past, but it is still a painful memory. She was more or less frigid, and his unsatisfied desire for her exhausted him spiritually and physically, but he could not leave her; only his separation from her by military service ended the affair. With much hesitation he penetrates to the heart of his memories of Rosa, only to find that he has then to write about his relationship with Kat. He married Kat because she was pregnant, but there was little passion in their affair, for she was thoroughly practical and down-to-earth. One night he lay pondering over the meaning of life: "Kat slept at my side. I stretched out my arms to infinity; it must have been a comic gesture in the dark. A strange gesture for an office worker. I don't know how it happened, but I discovered that Kat was a strange person and that I was in a strange house" (208). When Kat comes out to see him in the country and begs him to return, it becomes clear that they really are strangers. She cannot understand how he can throw up his job and social position and abandon his family, while he cannot understand that they are worth keeping: they give him no happiness, and they are destroying him as a human being.

Fax continues his life in the country, but although he lives peacefully he lives in rather a vacuum: "I have freedom but I have nothing to do with it" (231). Trivialities occupy his attention: insects, squirrels, hares, the smells and sounds of the forest, brief meetings and conversations. Such action as there is centers on a girl called Karin, whom Fax pursues in a languid fashion, watched jealously by Ceder, the local landowner, and Alf, an inarticulate farmhand. All three are involved in a love-hate relationship as rivals. Fax is involved as well in discussions with two visitors, Mårten Torpare—who also shows some interest in Karin—and an author known merely as E. J. "They quarrel almost all the time, but they could well be the same person, or two sides of the same person" (184), Fax notices.

Karin is a country girl, but no uninhibited child of nature like

Lydia in *Bobinack,* for she has spent some time in the town, and she reacts to Fax's theories of living for the moment by exclaiming: "Not everybody can think like that" (268). But her instincts are not perverted like those of Rosa, or rationalized away like those of Kat. Alf is a much more primitive being. His pet name Affe is also the German for "ape," and Fax usually refers to him as a dog, both because of his animal appearance and behavior and because of his dogged pursuit of his rival. But Affe too is tainted by urban civilization, or as Fax puts it: "I have sniffed at civilization and been slightly poisoned. Civilization has sniffed and looked at him and he has been a little poisoned by that" (113). Affe desires Karin, but dare not rape her for fear of the law. He hates Fax, but dare not murder him; he can only bite his hand, like a dog. And when Affe finds Karin has slept with Fax, in the rain at dawn, he drowns himself. Fax is bound to Affe by a kind of love: "Perhaps we are fond of one another in a grand, hateful way" (114). After his night with Karin, Fax confronts the beaten Affe and realizes how close the rivals are: "I become him, and he becomes me" (277). When Affe drowns himself, Fax tries to rescue him, and when he fails he mourns him, shutting himself off from the world, and letting his beard grow.

Fax is trying to discover and tell the truth about himself, but he finds the task not at all easy. The author E. J. is far from impressed by Fax's honesty, he tells him, and certainly Fax pursues a circuitous course in his narrative. Sometimes he finds a straightforward course impossible to pursue; when he comes to a delicate point in the past, he flees to the present: "When I am to write about myself I come across one thing after another where my will tells me to carry on, forward, but where something else lets me down. Not my memory. For example I can remember a lot about Rosa . . . . No, it's the passion for facts which stops, the desire to speak the truth. I consider quite simply that it's unnecessary. Passion relaxes, I seek other ways, the present" (134).

Ultimately, truth is a more complicated concept than it might appear. When Mårten tells Fax he must find out the truth about himself, Fax replies: "I tell myself now that to attain clarity about a number of things I must tell the truth. But the truth is that I can like something and be exhilarated by something today that I shall despise and loathe tomorrow" (62). Truth is relative to the observer and his state of mind. E. J. says of Fax's autobiography: "If someone were to write your wife's story we should have an equally true but quite different picture of you" (237). The concept of reality is similarly fluid. When Fax staggers home after a night's drinking with Ceder he sees the world transformed, and wonders if perhaps the world of his hangover is the real world, and the real world, the sober world, "only a terrible hangover" (121). Indeed, a greater perception of truth and reality—as one observer sees them—may be conveyed to others by falsification or unreality. E. J. tells an improbable story, but declares: "It is true in principle" (187). Ceder refers to Shakespeare's *A Winter's Tale* and the mention of the coast of Bohemia: "Bohemia has no seacoast where a real ship can run aground. It is only ships that are more than real, poetic ships, that can run aground there. They are laden with dreams; there are ghosts on board. Not until we lift it all up above reality does it come to life and become truth" (123).

A similar argument might be applied to *Rain at Dawn*. Fax's return to nature is somewhat fanciful, his night with Karin more lyrical than credible, but it does clearly illustrate an abstract argument: that man must show a greater openness to life, allow his instincts more rein than the tight control of society permits. Fax succeeds because he is hard-hearted, something which E. J. admires since it lends him "a kind of greatness" (233). He is able to abandon Kat, and he is quickly able to overcome his grief at Affe's death. But clearly Kat's point of view cannot be overlooked, and there is a dilemma that E. J. is well aware of: "We must have a better society, where people like you can have your rights—room for happiness. And where people like your wife needn't suffer. Actually, there is no absolute goal for man's strivings. Let us believe in the fight for better human beings. By better I don't mean those who are good in all circumstances, but those who are less inhibited, more open" (236–37).

III *In Defense of Democracy*

Johnson does not pursue the problem of a new society further. The Torpare series is interrupted by the novels about Olof (1934–37), and when Mårten Torpare reappears it is in quite different circumstances. *In Rain at Dawn* the author E. J. remarks: "My task is not to answer but to ask questions. Questions which others cannot formulate" (237). This is a repetition of Magnus Lyck's

realization in *Commentary on a Falling Star,* and can equally apply
to the author Eyvind Johnson in his tentatively phrased problem
novels of the early 1930s. But the rise of fascism seemed to demand
more definite formulations and points of view, and when Mårten
Torpare reappears in *Nattövning* (*Night Maneuvers,* 1938), it is as a
man with a clear and unequivocal message to deliver: resistance.

Mårten's change of heart is symbolically represented at the
beginning of *Night Maneuvers,* which opens with the funeral of an
actor famous particularly for his playing of Hamlet. It is a decisive
farewell to Hamlet and the luxury of disinterested enquiry. Now
the need is for action: "In our time Hamlet is something only an
actor can be in all seriousness, and yet he has to be Hamlet on a
stage. Perhaps there will come a time when he will rise from the dead,
not as a savior—he's not that type—but as a spirit among men,
devoted to life's problems" (6). The funeral is thus symbolic as the
car crash in *Bobinack* is, and it plays a similar role in the construction
of the novel, for the main characters are witnesses of the funeral
procession. And as in *Bobinack* the various characters are developed
to represent different attitudes to one idea, in this case Nazism.

The author seems particularly concerned to discover what type
of person is attracted to Nazi doctrines, and he portrays a range of
characters, from out-and-out Nazis to those who are unconscious
of their latent sympathies for the movement. Mårten Torpare goes
to a Nazi meeting in Sweden and describes the public as follows:
"A great many school children, old ladies, elderly gentlemen with
martial mustaches and the erect bearing of 1914; officers in civilian
clothes; some workers of the restless, mentally unbalanced, often
querulous strikebreaking type: rootless, despised, unhappy, venge-
ful" (113). The Nazi sympathizers in this and Johnson's later
novels are generally of this last type. Nazism offers them a sense of
self-importance, an opportunity for revenge, which consoles them
for what they see as personal injustices and the feeling that life
has treated them unfairly.

Such a character is Gideon Hannes. Mårten describes him as
being a little like Bobinack, but a weak Bobinack, "indecisively
nice and indecisively cruel" (37). In his youth he has been in the
United States, but has been attacked as a strikebreaker and made
lame. Back in Sweden he has set up as a builder but has been ruined
by a series of strikes. Rather than place the blame for his misfortunes on himself, he sees the cause as being an international con-

spiracy of Jews and Bolsheviks. He joins "The Group," a collection
of Nazis who plan to take over the government of Sweden and to
this end smuggle weapons into the country. In his activities for the
cause Gideon Hannes can forget his own personal inadequacies,
can ignore the fact that his behavior is in pathetic contrast to his
ideals of "Justice, Purity, Power" (55), that he is lame, that he has
suppressed homosexual tendencies, that he drinks. During the
"night maneuvers"—arms-smuggling—his car is pursued by the
police, and in the chase which ends in his death Gideon Hannes
achieves his ultimate self-fulfillment:

He is the triumphant part of a terrible, incomprehensible whole, but he
feels no fear, nor is he filled with courage. His feeling is of certainty. (229)

Gideon Hannes compensates for his failings in life by serving
a cause offering meaning and excitement. A relative of his, Bengt
Hannes, is a schoolboy who is attracted to the cause because it
appeals to his youthful idealism and because the leader of "The
Group," Kristian Nordblom, is a kind of father figure to him.
Nordblom is a rather indistinct character in the novel, possibly an
idealist, but possibly merely an opportunist. Mårten describes him
as: "A man who seems deeply disillusioned with life or has seen
his chance" (113). He has been a schoolteacher and has seduced—or
been seduced by—Nora Gyllem, then one of his pupils, but she has
rejected him as a lover. Indeed, sexual inadequacy or perversion is
as much a feature of the Nazis in the novel as is a more general
failure in life. Nora, who is now a twenty-nine-year-old woman of
a "decidedly erotic type" (13), is picked up by a German advisor
to "The Group," and he proves to be impotent.

Although few Swedes are as actively engaged in Nazism as "The
Group," Johnson indicates how vague sympathies lie just below
the surface in more passive characters. Nora's current lover is a
budding film star called Krister, a superficial character she treats
with some irony: "'I am an Arab, a Mongol, and a Negress,' she
said. 'Well, I haven't any racial prejudices,' he replied. He became
very serious: 'Anyway it's ridiculous to have prejudices of that
kind. I can say so although I'm pure Germanic, pure Aryan'" (17).
Krister's protestations, however unconvincing, show that he is at
least dimly aware of what is going on. Nora's foster parents, an
elderly, rather pathetic couple called Elvira and Jesper Hannes,

react to Nazi doctrines at a less conscious level. At the movies they see a film about the white slave trade, and Jesper is led to reflect on the poor white girls: "They danced for swarthy types, mestizos and bandits of the worst sort. No, they ought to put a stop to it! Perhaps all that stuff about races wasn't such a bad idea of the Germans. Anyway the white, the Nordic white race, was the best" (152). But his indignation is momentary, and he goes on to erotic fantasies about Negresses; like Krister, his ideas are superficial.

One side of the novel, then, is a study of active Nazi supporters and those who are ripe for conversion. The other side concerns the opposition to Nazism and is represented by Mårten Torpare and his friend Tomas Gyllem, Nora's husband. Tomas is an engineer and has specialized in the invention of weapons, but in one of his experiments four of his colleagues have been killed and so he has turned his back on armaments and become a pacifist. Now the years of idleness have finally proved too much for him. He feels he must start again with something, and he decides to leave Nora and set off on a journey. Caught in change and uncertainty, he meets Mårten and explains his problems to him. He feels that he *must* occupy himself with arms: "You discover that you've been going in the wrong direction . . . yet you feel your human dignity, your dignity as a creative individual *depends entirely on your continuing*" (141). Mårten, however, brushes aside Tomas's personal problems and talks about *real* suffering. Does Tomas realize what the Nazis' victims suffer in concentration camps, in torture chambers? And like Bobinack with Romaticus, Mårten gives Tomas a brutal, blow-by-blow account of the crucifixion of Christ. Tomas is moved, but his personal problems still continue to dominate him. Mårten perseveres, proclaiming himself to be "the destroyer of your deeply tragic feeling that life has kicked you wholly unjustly" (266). Personal preoccupations, be they ethical or esthetic, seem so irrelevant now: "Perhaps the essential thing now is that someone, an unknown, weak, perhaps even unattractive man, is lying behind a machine gun and defending the Spanish Republic" (260).

Still Mårten makes no impression on Tomas's self-pity and despair. But then Tomas stumbles on "The Group" stowing away their smuggled weapons in a cellar. He is coshed, bound, and left in the cellar. His sufferings are described in detail, and from this direct experience of only a tiny part of what the Nazis' victims suffer. Tomas understands that the Nazis and their like are his enemies and must be fought:

> I must help to preserve freedom. And for me there are not so many ways. There, in the cellar, I acquired a kind of certainty . . . . That I can kill. That I have some knowledge of killing. That I want to use what I know. That we can fight them—the cellar men—down there in Spain. There are doubtless many solutions to the same problem. This is mine. I am a detail the good forces in the world may make use of, extract the greatest usefulness from. (319)

Tomas decides to fight Nazism by military means, and he goes to Spain. Mårten determines to fight the menace in his way, by literary means. He is about to write a new book and he decides it must be different from such works as *Rain at Dawn:* "Perhaps too many people have walked in the forests in Scandinavian literature" (38). Instead it will be "a diary about what is happening now" (41). He considers his past theories: "A kind of faith in blood, in grass, in clouds, in rain, in uninhibited experience. How far away this was after a few years! 'The face of the world has changed so quickly,' he said. 'The individual's fate matters so little now'" (259). Seeing the monsters produced by men's instincts and irrational impulses, he qualifies his earlier primitivist beliefs: "The previously fresh springs, the mystic springs in the very depths of man, down in his darkness, his night ego, may be polluted and can be purified by reason, spirit" (41). The argument returns to Andersson's insistence in *Town in Darkness* that only a combination of reason and emotion, brain and heart, is a proper solution to man's problems. Tomas Gyllem echoes this when he thinks of the buried actor in his role as Hamlet: "When he held Yorick's skull in his hands you saw that it was also a brain, not merely a place for keeping things, but a brain. The thing that is closest to Spirit and may well be it—with the help of glands and canals from the little toe upwards" (7).

Reason tells Mårten that no decent society can emerge from Nazism. Nazism must be destroyed, and he comes to a terrible conclusion: "The mounting, bitter conviction that force might have to be met with force, that life is so fantastic that grenades must tear apart human bodies for mankind to achieve the possibility of happiness" (244). He attempts to understand the tremendous sacrifice that will be required of those like Tomas who take part in the struggle. Some may sacrifice happiness:

> But that is not the greatest sacrifice. A greater sacrifice is life itself with its possibility of feeling, of understanding both happiness and our own pride in being strong enough to sacrifice happiness. Life, with its possibility of peace beyond restlessness, honor beyond humiliation, victory after defeat. To die a personal, individual, lonely death, perhaps a painful death, conscious that the epitaph we get may be "Contempt." That is the great sacrifice of happiness for the sake of an unknown future. The very nature of this sacrifice is unhappiness; not merely a lack of happiness, but positive, enduring, eternal unhappiness—the direct opposite of happiness .... The greatest and most terrible sacrifice is to sacrifice your own death when you have sacrificed your personal, individual life. The officer dies his death, but perhaps his memory will be honored in the future, while the unknown soldier receives neither honor nor scorn, he sacrifices his death as he has sacrificed his life even before falling. And—Mårten hesitates— perhaps the victory of justice will be a victory in blood, a victory demanding just such unknown men who will not be heroes, who will not be anything, who will be dead and nameless.   (246–47)

The final Mårten Torpare novel, *Soldatens återkomst* (*The Soldier's Return*, 1940) is devoted to such a soldier, by the name of Sten. He calls himself "Scandinavia's Soldier," for Johnson emphasizes the shared beliefs of the Nordic countries and the necessity for their acting together to preserve their common civilization, just as Tomas Gyllem explains that his family originated in Norway, moved to Denmark, and finally settled in Sweden. Sten returns to a quiet Swedish village and is fatally assaulted. He is discovered in the middle of the summer night lying in the road, and the novel contrasts his experiences on Europe's battlefields, expressed as the memories passing through his feverish brain, with the trivial preoccupations of the villagers who gather round his death bed.

Many of the villagers' thoughts are concerned with a girl called Maria, who is in the tradition of other erotic women in the Torpare novels: Sigrid, Lydia, Karin, and Nora. But she is treated rather less sympathetically than her predecessors, obsessed as she is with self-pity: "All stretched out their hands for me and wanted to be together with me, but no one knew that I was like that, that I let them be with me because I felt so lonely. I lie here now and I am so lonely and no one can help me out of it" (148). Chief among the men she takes to relieve her loneliness is Sander, who has acquired an almost hypnotic hold over her. He is called Alexander "after a great warrior" (235), and he is a hardbitten criminal. He starts his career when a child by setting fire to his parents' cottage and making himself an orphan. As a man he takes to smuggling but is caught and imprisoned. He is convinced that he has been unjustly treated by fate, and he is driven by hate and feelings of revenge. It is Sander who strikes Sten because he has had an affair with Maria. Before Sten loses consciousness he recognizes in Sander the basic ingredients of the Nazi type: "It was The Enemy. It was the enemy I have met in my wars. It was a ravaged and hard face, and I read its inscription: it was frustration, envy, hate because of imagined injustice, lust for power, boastfulness, cowardice, cunning, and ultimately a bottomless dread" (312).

A rather different character, who follows Maria as slavishly as she follows Sander, is the village shopkeeper, Berntson. He is middle-aged, physically unattractive, with limited interests, who has little to offer Maria but security. In other circumstances he would be a harmless man, but in the shadow of war his preoccupation with Maria seems reprehensible. When Berntson and Mårten walk together, the former engrossed in thoughts of Maria, the latter overwhelmed by what is happening in the rest of Europe, Mårten thinks: "Plague and pestilence creep like worms and sail like vultures towards Scandinavia; and if you ask that man there what he thinks of it all, he'll stare at you and say—what?" (262).

Not all men, though, are like Sander or like Berntson. A more appealing character is Elias Lundström, a young army recruit. He too has been involved with Maria, but he has seen through her self-pity: "You could never chat with her. She made up a lot of stuff about how lonely she was and how she needed sympathy. She wanted to be cuddled" (182). His ambitions are not, like Sander's, criminal, or, like Berntson's, to be reckoned in money. He is creative, likes working with cars and gardening. He is aware too of the more vital problems in the world, and he is ready to defend Sweden from occupation if the need arises.

While the actual story occupies only a few hours in the early morning, the characters are presented in depth through their memories, through what are essentially monologues. Their activities are punctuated by Sten's story, told in four monologues. He has

fought in Spain, Finland, and Norway, but he sees these campaigns
as a continuous struggle: "The bullet in Spain opened the vessel
that is my body, so that my blood could then run out on the soil
of Finland and Norway" (35). It is irrelevant whether the enemy
is Franco, Stalin, or Hitler, or even Sander—their characteristics
are the same, and they have nothing to offer mankind. Sten sees
mankind's salvation as "decency" in life's sometimes tortuous
relationships. His enemies offer only hate and vengeance.

For Mårten the day on which Sten is killed has a more private
significance: it is his fortieth birthday, just as it also happens to
be Eyvind Johnson's. The night before, he has taken stock of his
life: "Living at your age is not only being alive and going round
seeing faces and experiencing events. It is just as much remembering"
(196). Remembering is a process of excavation, which Mårten
compares to the excavation of Troy. Layer after layer of time is
exposed, but then everything becomes confused, just as a rainstorm
swept objects from different layers of Schliemann's excavations
into one trench. Memories are all jumbled up, man's soul is confusion. But one thing stands out clearly to Mårten, that he cannot
live if dictatorship triumphs, if freedom is destroyed. The clouds
gather, the future is unpromising: "But further away, on the
horizon, we see something else, in smoke and hope. Over there a
great island nation is fighting for us and the Western World" (202).

In the Mårten Torpare novels Johnson is very determinedly
the novelist of ideas. His plots, when they exist, are simple and
undistracting; his characters—with the exception of Bobinack—
stereotyped, their emotional lives circumscribed by the demands
of the argument. Within his chosen limits Johnson displays technical skill, and he can write passages of controlled intensity—such
as Mårten's reflections on the sacrifice of both life and memory
after death—and of idyllic lyricism, as in *Rain at Dawn*. But as far
as the 1930s are concerned, the Torpare novels are completely
overshadowed by *The Novel About Olof*, which will now be discussed.

CHAPTER 4

Portrait of an Author

I The Novel About Olof

EASILY the most successful story in Johnson's first book, *The Four Strangers*, is "Vallberg," about an amusement-stall owner in Norrbotten. Strangely enough, Johnson did not immediately continue to exploit the subject matter of his childhood province, for although *Town in Darkness* and *Remembering* are set in the north of Sweden, the characters are not specifically Norrbotten people. A vast reservoir of childhood and adolescent memories of a beautiful and desolate province remained to be tapped. The process began after the author had moved to Saint-Leu-la-Forêt in 1927: "In St. Leu I made my living to some extent by writing short stories of the postwar period for Swedish newspapers. The short stories, the sketches, were, to begin with, set in Germany and France, the true countries of postwar people. Then their already twisted nature was further distorted. Slowly, but without serious opposition, they changed into people from Norrbotten. Out of it all, out of my own confusion, the Norrbotten short stories *burst* forth."[1]

A comparison of the short stories written in France and Germany (largely to be found in *The Night Has Come*) with those set in Norrbotten (in *Once More, Captain* and *The Secure World*) shows how much more life and color there is in the Norrbotten stories. Not only that: Johnson shows a warm sympathy for his Norrbotten characters. Certainly he can laugh at them, at the hero of "Difficult Hour" for example, who refrains from hanging himself because the site is unsuitable, or at the alcoholic captain in the title story of *Once More, Captain*, who dreams of his days on the oceans of the world while he steers a tiny lake steamer on an erratic course. But the laughter is not the cold mockery that sometimes dominates the early novels. In dealing with these characters Johnson showed a depth of feeling he had rarely revealed in his previous works. When he returned to his own childhood, in the tetralogy *Romanen*

om Olof (*The Novel About Olof,* 1934–37), and to the railroad laborers he had grown up among, he realized that the railroad worker was
"a typical figure from the Swedish people, the *fine* Swedish people
. . . the Swedish people at its very best." [2]

The first volume of *The Novel About Olof, Nu var det 1914* (*Now
It was 1914,* 1934), begins just before the fourteenth birthday of
its young hero, Olof Persson. Olof makes a determined break with
his childhood by leaving first his foster parents and then, when he
comes home, his real parents. From these farewells and the memories
they arouse in him, a picture of his childhood emerges, a picture
of isolation and loneliness. Olof's father, a former railroad worker,
had fallen ill—some kind of mental illness—when Olof was young,
and the boy had been handed over to foster parents to ease the mother's financial difficulties. When Olof comes home he sees his family
as strangers, yet he cannot accept his foster parents as real parents.
Instead he feels weighed down by the obligation to show them
gratitude. His sense of spiritual separation from his family is
matched by a physical isolation. His foster parents live in the middle
of desolate marshlands, where the iron-ore railroad is the only
link with the outside world. Olof is always on his own, whether it
be on his winter hunting expeditions or in his games in summer,
when he has to call out the names of imaginary playmates. There
is no warmth or companionship up there; even laughter is strange:
"He used to laugh only when he was alone. He practiced laughing,
as it were, in case he should have cause for laughing later on" (10).

His farewell to all this is understandable, but it is scarcely a
conscious decision for him: "His departure was sudden, yet obstinately determined. It was as if he himself had no say in the matter
and merely followed the whim to leave" (14). He starts work, and
his first job is sorting timber at a timber boom. The work is really
too hard for him, an all too abrupt initiation into manhood, but the
others at the boom scarcely notice, for they started the same way:
"They have never had time to be children, youths; they have always
been workers" (80). However, Olof senses that his life will not ultimately be like theirs. He meditates as he rests in the light northern
night:

Olof looks shyly at the men, but he cannot become friends with them.
So many years between. One day I may be like them, he thinks. But he
knows immediately that his life will not be like theirs, it is a conviction, he

knows it definitely, firmly, intensely. His back aches from the toil out on the mass of timber, his hands have acquired blisters and wheals from the handle of the boat hook, his head is dizzy from the strange atmosphere, a dream atmosphere between sleep and waking. Their voices are loud and clear, all sounds are magnified. The roar of the river is a distant train, coming and coming and never arriving. The night is broad and light, it has no real darkness. He cannot find any word for it other than that it is broad and light. A broad frontier, this summer 1914, when childhood is torn out of his body. He lies with his cheek against the cool grass, and the blood beats at his temples. Fear and joy, tiredness and strength. (69)

There is little to justify Olof's faith in a different future. Although he escapes from the timber boom to a brick kiln, and later starts potato picking, his burden of work scarcely lessens. He has no time to play or relax; he has to go from being a child to being a man without a break. Throughout the book he balances uneasily between childhood and youth: "When he was alone he could say that he wasn't a child . . . . 'I am no longer a child, I am a worker.' But if someone had called him a child he could not have denied it. It was like a crime he had been discovered committing, something to be ashamed of" (153). For example, Olof plays soccer football with the potatoes he is picking, then suddenly realizes his behavior is childish. At work he must use his adult fellow workers' language, but when on his own he uses a language with children's words in it. Alone in the barracks at night, he is overwhelmed by fear of the dark: "a darkness which made him afraid and small against his will" (219).

Now It Was 1914 is a farewell to childhood. The most obvious end of childhood is the physical labor forced on Olof, "when childhood is torn out of his body." Yet he is not crushed, for at the end he still looks to the future; when he overcomes his fear of the dark he feels "an ecstasy of reality, he was wide open to his life" (235). The sexual changes of puberty are only dimly perceived, near the end of the novel. Olof looks into the eyes of a young shop girl and she looks at him "motherly-sisterly, yet not motherly-sisterly" (227). And at the very end of the novel: "Suddenly he remembered the girl who had leant forward and looked into him. And he felt a wild longing for her. He didn't want to turn back, but have her here, talk with her, touch her hand, face, neck, ask her name. And so his childhood was over" (238).

The author largely adopts Olof's point of view in the novel, and

consequently the story is limited by Olof's own limitations and
expands as Olof himself broadens his outlook. The war raging in
the rest of Europe does not interest Olof and so plays no part in
the novel. Similarly, the economic system that is responsible for
the inhuman conditions the fourteen-year-old has to work in is
not openly criticized in the first of the Olof books, for Olof is too
young to understand it. Only in one section does the author attempt
to express something outside Olof's range of experience, and that
is when he tries to give a wider picture of life in Norrbotten. He
does this by means of a *saga*, "fairy tale." Each of the four Olof
novels contains a fairy tale, and in the first three volumes the fairy
tale has no obvious point of contact with the novel. In a postscript
to the last Olof book, *Finale in Youth*, Johnson explains his reasons
for adopting this technique: "If one decides to try to describe a
province or a person as fully as possible, one must work with considerable freedom. If the author's attempts to give a complete
picture falter before an often depressing reality, which seems to
him so dismal that he puts down his pen and merely sits staring
into nothingness, then he can take a roundabout route via the
fairy tale. The fairy tale is always an open door" (388).

   The reality of life in Norrbotten is harsh and depressing, and
fairy tales offer a more attractive approach to the subject. Yet
they are essentially true, for all their extravagance and fantasy.
When he leaves home Olof meets a storyteller on the train: "For
Olof he was a teller of fairy tales. His reality was a fairy tale, and
everything emerging from his mouth became fairy tales. 'I would
like to be like that,' Olof thought" (50–51). Olof's control of language is not yet sufficient for him to tell stories, and the fairy tale
in *Now It Was 1914* is told by another character for whom reality
has to be transformed by fantasy, a man called Klack. Klack
claims, for example, that his father was bewitched by an attractive
sorceress but was cured by a mercury bullet in his thigh; or in other
words that he contracted venereal disease and was given an injection.
His fairy tale is called "The Tale of Tuberculosis and the Mist."
Tuberculosis was an extremely widespread disease in Norrbotten
at the time, and it is not surprising that Johnson should feel some
hesitation in approaching the subject. Klack makes a fable out of
it all. His twin sons, he announces, died of tuberculosis after being
bewitched by a whirlwind. His wife, on her way across the meadow
to the well, breathes in the germs with the mist, and in the mist

she hears the voices of her dead children. They call to her to join them in heaven, while a voice from earth begs her to remain. Bewildered by the dialogue she sinks to the ground, and her life's memories flash across her mind: a phonograph she has seen, a book she has read, a young forester she almost had an affair with. The fairy tale combines the description of a simple but moving life with a sophisticated technique. Sometimes the narrator is Klack, sometimes the author intervenes, while Klack's wife uses her own peculiar language with its half-remembered biblical allusions, her only cultural contact, to present her thoughts. And in a fever her thoughts, and the elements of the story, are mixed up in a stream of consciousness (139).

Fairy tales dominate the second part of the Olof series, *Här har du ditt liv* (*Here You Have Your Life,* 1935). There is little action in the novel, which is set in the winter 1915–16. It opens with Olof, now employed at a sawmill, attending his father's funeral, and it ends with Olof rebelling against his boss and leaving the sawmill. The real interest centers on Olof's intellectual development, and the cultural environment from which he develops.

Olof finds his fellow workers at the sawmill resigned and apathetic, but he is not content to be like them. He begins reading, partly as an escape from his tedious life, but partly too as a way of getting something better, through knowledge. The others regard his books with suspicion, but Olof has a strength of purpose and a moral backbone that they lack. In so far as they have any notion of morality it is that of slaves scared of an omnipresent god's watchful eye and grim punishment. Olof, however, has inherited a moral code that places responsibility on the individual. He is answerable to himself for his words and actions, even if the Devil himself should stand there and threaten him: "It is the finest morality that has ever existed, this morality of railroad builders, and it is hard; it is not so easily learned or taught, no, it has to lie in man's heart, *be in his blood.* The Devil stands there, tempting and threatening. He is cunning and cruel, and it is no use clinging to your mother's skirts or your father's coat. *You are alone*" (76). Olof reveals his independence and determination when he stands up to the sawmill owner at the end of the novel, resists his conciliatory gestures, and leaves: "You are you. It's you who are you. You must try to stand on your own feet and eat your own food. You must not live off others" (282).

The development of Olof's moral sense is paralleled by his increasing intellectual awareness. To begin with he is limited by his
vocabulary, and he finds he knows things without being able to
express them. For example, when he thinks about his fellow workers'
use of swear words:

> Olof hit on the truth about swear words early on. Not here. He knew it
> before from experience, although a long time was to pass before he could
> clothe it in comprehensible words. He sat so deep down amongst *the
> people* and so near the bottom from which everything is churned up that
> his sight was not clear, and there was no possibility for him of an overall
> view. But in later years he often discovered things he had known before,
> in fact had always known. When he saw Larsson and Johansson he *knew*
> what they were like, and what man on earth was like. But he could not have
> said it, described them, talked about what he knew with anyone else.
> (114–15)

Olof's development from a more or less illiterate boy to a youth
able to express his thoughts and observations is perhaps the most
important theme of the tetralogy. In *Here You Have Your Life,*
Olof reads indiscriminately and his impressions are presented in
all their confusion: "Read *Leisure* because knowledge is power.
If you read a lot you become mad. Submit to your fate, work, and
do not despair. You should never be satisfied; to be satisfied is to
be dead and no longer want things. Be alone and strong. To be alone
is treachery against the masses. Only man has value. Man is spirit.
Man is only part of nature, an insignificant part. Man is a kind of
ape, an older ape, a variant of ape. Man is soul" (252–53). This
is as far as Olof comes in this novel; he must sort his ideas into some
order later.

Books are a means to material advancement and intellectual
development, but as much as anything they are an escape from
an often intolerable reality. Flight from reality is the major theme
of *Here You Have Your Life.* It applies to Olof's fellow workers:
"There is a small quantity of dreams in their lives. There is little
clarity in them, and that is good for them, in a way good. The
moment they stood up, put their hands to their breasts and said,
'Now I see clearly'—that moment would be their last. They would
not be able to bear the terrible truth: that their lives are a rubbish
dump, that their lives are a frozen or sweaty hell and nothing else"
(38–39). Olof finds himself living in two worlds: the world of the

sawmill, with aching back and blistered hands, and a world of dreams and fairy tales when he lies in his bunk at night. He ponders on the fairy tales such escapism has produced in Norrbotten: "They are a kind of fairy tale which could scarcely come from any other province. There is a great deal of reality in them, almost everything is reality, it is only the tone that must be that of a fairy tale so that it does not all become dreary and depressing everyday life" (144).

One of the fairy tales in *Here You Have Your Life* is the story of a farmer who makes a fortune selling his forests to a company. With the money he buys an organ and abandons his farm to devote himself to music and dreams. The story is told as a plot of God and the Devil to test the poor man's soul. His hold on reality weakens, and he retires into his own private world, overwhelmed by unreality. Perhaps his story is meant as a comment on Olof's father, who had similarly lost contact with the outside world. The main fairy tale in the book is about the farmer's daughter, Johanna, who is also destroyed by too much fantasy. "The Tale of Johanna" is told partly as a folk ballad, in rhymed, sentimental verse and partly in cold prose. The contrast between the two narratives only emphasizes the necessity of making a ballad of the wretched girl's fate. Johanna, a sturdy and plain peasant girl, is seduced by a young vagrant, who immediately abandons her. But she sees him as a knight, whom fate has cruelly snatched from his fair lady. She wanders off to look for him, and meets him, but he quickly disappears again. She goes to pieces after this. Finally she comes across him as he is planning a crime, and since she knows too much, he shoots her: "This was fate, inevitable fate, and it smelt of misery and sex and blood. Dirt and a dream of the eternal, pure and clear golden light were mixed in her life. She was a maiden and a princess and a slave girl and Cinderella and the Goose Girl, a fairy and a doormat people wipe their feet on when they enter respectable houses. And she was The Poem, The Song—everything. She bore part of mighty Norrbotten in her and with her out into the world" (235).

The third volume of the series, *Se dig inte om* (*Don't Look Back*, 1936), is full of action. Spring is in the air—spring, 1916—and Olof has a permanent job in a cinema. It is easy work in comparison with his previous jobs, and he has more time and energy to read and to meet people. Two people who play a particularly important

part in his story are a waitress, Maria, and a happy-go-lucky young
fellow by the name of Fredrik. Olof becomes interested in Maria,
and she gives him some encouragement, but then she suddenly
leaves town. Olof cycles off to visit her, only to find her in the
company of another boy. He reacts by withdrawing into himself,
feeling very sorry for himself and at the same time sure he is superior
to all around him. In Fredrik, Olof acquires his first real friend.
Fredrik is full of tall stories and fantastic experiences, and Olof
easily sees through him, but he is at any rate someone Olof can talk
to. They argue about what they are going to do when The Revolution comes; they go swimming. However, as in *Here You Have Your
Life,* the reality behind the fantasy is grim, and always ready to
break through. Fredrik contracts venereal disease, not from any
of the romantic women he has talked about, but from a prostitute,
and his first sexual contact at that.

Fredrik needs money, and he asks Olof to help him by stealing
some oil. At first Olof refuses, but the claims of friendship and
the call of adventure prove too strong, especially in the general
atmosphere of moral relaxation in wartime Sweden. Olof sets out
in the dead of night, but on the way his attention is diverted by a
graveyard; and there he experiences a feeling of overwhelming
fear which completely destroys his will and his ability to think.
It is a fear that seems to come from the very beginnings of mankind,
a terror that is in man's blood, deep down in his inherited experiences. Olof finally exorcizes the fear by forming conscious
thoughts, asserting rational man's supremacy over irrational fear
and his own individuality against a universal force. But he will in
future always be aware of the dark powers that are latent in man:

> It's you who are you. And inside you and part of you is something else,
> something old, witchcraft, paganism, the dead you have never seen and
> the fear that will rise in men's souls again in a hundred or a thousand
> years' time, when things have come full circle. But it's you who are you.
> In the future you will walk on streets of stone and asphalt in large cities
> with tall houses, and you won't forget that witchcraft is in your blood.
> You're a chip of wood in the swelling waves, and it's you and no one
> else who is the chip.   (258–59)

After this, Olof recovers his self-respect sufficiently to turn his
back on theft, declaring: "They could look for someone else if they
wanted their oil stolen . . . . Though he could steal oil for a wage

of one crown twenty-five per hour. Be employed as an oil thief and get a pension when he was sixty-five, with his picture in the paper. 'In his prime he was one of the country's finest and most successful oil thieves'" (261–62).

While much of *Don't Look Back* is devoted to events and meetings, Olof's intellectual development is not neglected. His thoughts are still a hopeless hotchpotch of all he has read, but he is in the process of acquiring a greater control and awareness of words. For example, in his attempt to describe the countryside: "He had to say the countryside was really pretty. Or not pretty; the word didn't fit. But it was kind of attractive. Or not that either. It was— anyway, there was nothing wrong with the countryside" (23). Not only is Olof beginning to choose between synonyms, but he also composes his first fairy tale in this volume, a nonsense dream about three old women. From the passive stage of listening to stories he is proceeding to the active stage of creation.

The author's own fairy tale in this novel is "The Tale of the Country of Brazil." It concerns the emigration of Swedes to the American continent, but not the North American emigration later described in Vilhelm Moberg's famous tetralogy. Here it is the less well-known story of the Swedes who were enticed to Brazil, and it is told with a strong tone of social criticism and indignation which is otherwise absent in the Olof books. The emigrants left for Brazil believing it to be a land of enormous wealth and easy living. When they got there they found poverty, malaria, and poisonous snakes and spiders. This story of exploitation is redeemed only by the solidarity of their former comrades back home, who use their union funds to bring the survivors back. Once again, fantasy collides with reality.

The final volume of the Olof series is *Slutspel i ungdomen* (*Finale in Youth*, 1937), which begins in the fall of 1917 and ends in 1919 when Olof again takes leave of his foster parents, this time to leave Norrbotten completely. In this volume Olof is much preoccupied with "human dignity." He refuses to let himself be humiliated or ordered about by his employers. At the beginning of the novel he is sacked by the cinema owner for distributing socialist news-papers, and when the owner relents and asks Olof to stay he refuses. He has a variety of jobs afterwards, but he often finishes up by attempting to organize a strike and being dismissed. He becomes deputy secretary in the local branch of a trade union organization

and attempts to enroll his fellow workers: he is sure the revolution
is just round the corner. But Olof's pure revolutionary thoughts
are distracted by personal problems. He meets Olivia, "Queen
Olivia," who owns a shooting gallery, and he becomes hopelessly
involved in a love-hate relationship with her. She is, unfortunately,
a nymphomaniac, and her repeated infidelity drives him away,
until once again he takes up with her. Industrial strife and erotic
conflict exert their destructive powers on poor Olof. He becomes
drunk one evening, then another evening and another. He is unable
to find work, and he lives at home off his family. He attempts to
cycle south, but his bicycle collapses. Altogether, Olof seems
to be in the process of destroying himself, yet somehow he pulls
through. The philosophy that more than anything else helps him
to survive is "the deep tone": "There is only one human being, and
that is you. And then there are all the other human beings. You
belong to them. Everyone is alone, and you can never get through
to the others; and all belong together and are humanity, and you
belong to that" (341).

Finale in Youth is characterized by its intimate blending of
literature and life. Literature colors Olof's interpretation of his
experiences, while his experiences in their turn are expressed through
literature. When Olof tramps through the snow on his way to work,
he thinks of the *Anabasis* and the Greeks' encounter with snow in
the Armenian mountains. In a section entitled "Life via Literature"
Olof sees the dawn in Homeric terms as "The Maiden of the Morn,
rosy-fingered Eos" (50), while his work as a laborer on a building
site is seen as an incident in a historical novel, full of archaisms.
Olof's involvement in literature and the breadth of his reading are
perfectly illustrated in the fairy tale in this volume, which takes
the form of a fevered dream Olof experiences when he lies ill with
the Spanish flu. The story is entitled "The Tale of the Land of the
Pleasures of the Soul and the Vanity of the Spirit," or "Meeting
with the Spanish Girl," a simpler title expressing both the cause
of the dream and its contents. For in the dream Olof meets Olivia in
a variety of literary roles: Vicomte Olof of Ultima Thule in a Dumas
novel, Buffalo Olof of the Wild West, Olof Hamlet, Olof Werther,
King Olof of the Sagas, Olof Odysseus. Even the literary style is
imitated: blank verse for Hamlet, hexameters for Homer. Literature, the dream indicates, is as much a part of Olof's experiences
as his more directly acquired knowledge. He has his dreary life as

a laborer, but he also lives in a land where all dreams and pleasures are fulfilled, and a land that he can display to others as a mark of his superiority, a land won out of spiritual vanity.

Finally, Olof is himself a creator of literature. His actual works may be no more than poems read out to the assembled comrades at union meetings, but verbal self-expression is becoming something of a necessity for him. When he revisits his home he finds himself speechless: "I sit here and they can get nothing out of me. I have no words now. Later on I'll get words, *otherwise I can't live!*" (28). When he prepares to leave Norrbotten, he takes stock of his life:

> You didn't know how it was going to turn out, for there wasn't a good plan to follow. Everything you'd experienced of the future was dreams, and many were stupid. Odd, he thought, that I've never seen a windmill, though I know exactly what they're like. And really I know what men were like five hundred years ago, although I've never met anyone from then. In actual fact he knew a lot, though of course he had to find out the words for it. That was it: finding out the words for what you actually knew. There were no directions you could use. You had to begin by finding out. Finding out words. (385)

"Finding out words"—this is a writer's ambition; and it is difficult to forget what Olof's double, young Eyvind Johnson, has developed into, difficult not to see the story as that of a boy breaking his way out of an unpromising environment to become an international novelist. Yet it is important to notice that nothing of this is hinted at in the Olof novels, as it is in the autobiographical novels discussed in the next section. Nothing is said about Olof's future. Something else it is difficult not to read into the novels is the atmosphere of Norrbotten: its long dark winters, its light summers, its great rivers, its desolate marshes. There is actually little of this in the novels, even in the first two volumes. What Johnson describes of Norrbotten is its people's dreams, their longings, their fairy tales—the veils of fantasy they hold up in front of a reality that for them is not romantic but harsh and cruel. What Johnson essentially describes in *The Novel About Olof* is adolescence, a boy's development from child to man. Certainly Olof is Olof, a special person in special circumstances, but he is also every other adolescent: "all belong together and are humanity."

II   *Two Romantic Tales*

Something of a continuation to *The Novel About Olof* is provided
by a two-volume novel written nearly two decades later. The
first volume is *Romantisk berättelse* (*Romantic Tale*, 1953) and
the second is *Tidens gång* (*The Course of Time*, 1955), which is
subtitled *En romantisk berättelse (A Romantic Tale)*. It is a work
of quite a different kind from the Olof books, in quite a different
setting. Just as the Olof books spring from Johnson's experiences
in Norrbotten during his adolescence, so *Romantic Tale* and *The
Course of Time* continue his autobiographical investigations
with his Continental experiences of the 1920s.

Like much of Johnson's postwar work the story is enacted on
more than one time plane. The narrator, Yngve Garans, describes
his actual writing of the novel in Switzerland in 1952–55, while
the story he is telling takes place thirty years earlier. An additional
complication is that the story is told by several different writers,
for Yngve has received a bundle of letters and diaries from his
cousin Greger Garans, and he incorporates these into his own
story, which is based on memory. This rather roundabout construction—memories combined with contemporary documents,
all set thirty years in the past—would seem to be dictated by a
feeling that an author cannot really reproduce the exact sentiments
of his younger self. As Yngve asks: "How am I to conduct the
dialogue between my younger and my older self? After all, it's
not the same person talking. It's at least two people . . . . The
younger self will become the older, but in maturing he will lose part
of the most sensitive apparatus in his machinery for expressing
and comprehending things" (II, 222–23).[3] Consequently the novels
are as much as anything a discussion of how the story is written.
The events of the 1920s are interrupted by Yngve's life in the 1950s,
or become so vivid that they actually become part and parcel of the
1950s; and the 1920s are determined by the erratic nature of
the elder Yngve's memory. He takes up a subject, then drops it,
or postpones it, or evades it. Events towards the end of the work
are foreshadowed at the beginning, as Yngve makes his way tentatively to the heart of the matter, hidden in past time. He remarks:
"'It was like this—.' No, it was not like that. It was quite different.
I don't know yet what it was like, but perhaps I shall find out. I
know though how it ended" (I, 13).

Yngve's story is that of a group of young Swedes who arrive on a chaotic Continent in the aftermath of the First World War. There, in Berlin and Paris, they attempt to find their bearings. There is Yngve himself, who begins a career as a writer with a good education behind him and a private income. His friend Olle Oper also wants to be a writer, but he comes from a working-class background, without formal education or money. His story is told largely through his letters to a similarly situated young writer in Stockholm —Klas-Henrik—and his diaries. It is the story of a budding author's persistent attempts to gain recognition despite heartbreaking setbacks, and of his intellectual development via such men as Freud, Proust, and Joyce. Olle is particularly engaged in the anarcho-syndicalist movement, and in this he is contrasted with Greger Garans, who comes to the Continent as a spoiled and superficial young man but develops into one who is politically very much aware of what is happening. The three men—Yngve, Olle, and Greger— are all involved with a girl called Hedvig. Unlike the men she does not survive the emotional stresses of Berlin and Paris and eventually she commits suicide.

All these characters remain in a sense shadows. Perhaps it is significant that the successor to Olof Persson is called Olle Oper: Olle is a familiar form of Olof, while Oper, Greger suggests, could be short for *opersonligt,* "impersonal" (I, 95), as opposed to *Persson,* "person." For Olof has certainly become impersonal. One example: Although he gets married in the course of the story, nothing is said about his wife or his relationship to her. The characters, it seems, are meant to represent moods and attitudes from the 1920s; they stand for a decade rather than have any life of their own. Ultimately they lose their separate identities, for in a dream at the end of the work Yngve sees himself, Greger, and Olle in front of him, and he says: "I began to walk faster. When I came nearer I saw them merge into one another, or it may have been an effect of the light or the dark which made it appear so. Finally it seemed to me they had become a single, rather misty figure, formed from the twilight with some light in it. It seemed to me that the figure was most like Olle" (II, 472).

Discretion no doubt contributes to this approach to the subject. Johnson is using living, identifiable models in this work and must clearly be careful about what he says. One of the themes of the book is, in fact, the question of an author's responsibility towards those who provide the material for his works. An English authoress, Lucy D., strides through *The Course of Time* in search of likely material and duly places Hedvig in a short story. This story seems to be the immediate cause of Hedvig's suicide; when her body is discovered, a copy of the story lies beside it. But even if discretion lies behind the rather disembodied nature of the novels, this very abstractness is the artistic principle on which they are constructed. Yngve bases his technique on that of music, a subject he returns to again and again in the novel. He does not try to imitate musical form in the way Aldous Huxley does in *Point Counter Point* for example. When Yngve describes music it is in emotional, not formal, terms; in terms of light and darkness, peace and unease, as at the beginning of *Romantic Tale* (I, 7). The novels are likewise to be seen as contrasts in moods, with an uneasy balance between hope and despair. This is indicated by the two most frequently played pieces in the novels, which are Beethoven's piano sonatas Opus 2, No. 1 and, in particular, Opus 57 ("The Appassionata"); and most of all by the quotation from a book about the piano sonatas that prefaces *The Course of Time*: "Peace and gentleness do not triumph—but then do horror, black fear? . . . " (II, 7). Much of Johnson's work and many of his characters are in the state of unstable equilibrium characterized by this motto.

CHAPTER 5

Johannes Krilon

I *The Story*

IT is difficult for the re-narrator, the writing observer, to follow step by step all the paths running in and out of this story about Krilon," the author confesses in the second volume of his *Krilon* books (310). The rich and varied nature of the trilogy is no less bewildering for the reader than the author, but the 1,800 pages of *Grupp Krilon* (*Krilon's Group,* 1941), *Krilons resa* (*Krilon's Journey,* 1942), and *Krilon själv* (*Krilon Himself,* 1943) offer to the persevering the reward of what is not only Johnson's most imaginative work but also perhaps his most human.

The story concerns Johannes Krilon, a Stockholm estate agent. When the story opens at the beginning of 1941 he is a short, portly bachelor of forty-four. The son of a doctor, he had originally intended to follow his father's profession, but a cataclysmic experience changed his plans. At the age of twenty-four he went with his girl friend to celebrate midsummer on an island in Lake Mälaren, and there she was seduced by somebody else. His reaction was at first violent:

> I thought I should hate all my life. I hated her at least a month, and I hated her so much that I didn't become what I should have become. I didn't become a doctor. I hated her so much that I wanted to destroy mankind. Afterwards I only despised mankind for its weakness and wretchedness and because men were so easily blinded by falsehoods. But I couldn't keep up this contempt either, it didn't suit me.   (II, 348–49)[1]

The final result of this process is a man who is "mild, tolerant and reflective" (I, 40), with a firm belief in man's potential goodness and greatness, though without illusions about man's capacity for evil.

Together with six friends Krilon has formed a discussion group, "Krilon's Group," which meets every Sunday evening to exchange ideas and views. The members are: Hovall, a restorer of antique furniture, a tall meditative man addicted to snuff; his partner Minning, a shy widower, somewhat slow and melancholy, and devoted to his little daughter; Frid, a builder, who has worked his way up from nothing to become rich and successful; Odenarp, an electrical engineer, who is obsessed with the need for order and discipline in life; Arpius, a commercial traveler, whose life is bedeviled by an on-again-off-again affair with a hotel cashier; and Segel, a surgeon, the intellectual and cynic in the group.

The story begins with Krilon's taking a walk over the icebound Lake Mälaren. On his walk he passes the island where he had once celebrated that fateful midsummer, and shortly afterwards he passes a woman he recognizes as the girl concerned in the incident. He is led to reflect on the role it all played in his development, and at a meeting of the group that night he substitutes for the subject they had originally intended discussing—"Power and Powers"—the theme "The Significance of Tragedy." The new subject proves too difficult for the group; either they do not realize that personal tragedies can have any great significance, or else they lack the courage to talk about them. The original subject might have helped them more, for shortly afterwards Krilon is attacked by powers in the real-estate market whose aim is to achieve more power for themselves. These business rivals—G. Staph and T. Jekau in alliance—try to isolate Krilon by alienating the affections of his friends. They do this by spreading rumors about him and discrediting him, and by threatening and blackmailing. Gradually Krilon's friends turn against him, and they are particularly susceptible to outside pressure because of their own inward disarray after a series of personal tragedies: a result of tragedy they had not understood when Krilon had tried to warn them. Immersed in their own problems they have no time for others' difficulties and one by one they fall away. Frid discovers that his wife is having an affair with the butler, and he leaves home. Krilon immediately organizes a search for him on the basis of "the principle of sticking together" (I, 260), a principle the others feel is tiresome and impractical. During the search Hovall gets drunk and has a vision in which he is told by Jekau, who is ultimately indistinguishable from Staph, that Krilon is a menace: "He is trying to brake the dynamic progress of events and to fool you and everybody else into thinking that if you have might you shouldn't use it, and so on. And he comes along and talks about such antiquated things as *right,* without any might behind it!" (I, 323). Jekau's business methods are totally different, and his appeal is not to people's reason but to their deep, irrational instincts, as in his conversion of Hovall:

Hovall opened his eyes again, and then he saw something quite incredible. Mr. Jekau's rage had gone so far that he threw himself down on the floor and fastened his teeth in the carpet. Although Hovall tried to resist it he couldn't help being impressed by this intensely superhuman act. He hesitated as he sat in his armchair and felt an intoxication that no longer came from spirits and wine but from the half-converted's awakening to admiration for *action.* He suddenly felt that this unrestrained, forceful chewing of the carpet was one of the most important pieces of proof against Krilon that Mr. Jekau had presented . . . . He didn't think. He felt. He felt: "If I think now I'm lost!"   (I, 329)

The way in which Minning is won over from Krilon is similarly emotional and irrational, though it is fear that is the driving force. Minning's daughter is kidnapped by Staph, but as the result of a strange piece of brainwashing Minning somehow comes to feel that it is Krilon's fault. The personal tragedy cows him and drives him into himself, away from the others. For Segel personal tragedy proves altogether too great to bear. His ex-wife, with whom he is still very much in love, dies after an operation. Krilon tries to assemble the group to visit Segel and console him, but the others refuse to "interfere." Krilon goes on his own, but he is brusquely rejected by Segel. Shortly afterwards Segel commits suicide.

Krilon tries hard to hold the group together in adversity, but the members are impressed by the enemy's talk of action and a dynamic reorganization of society, and they are impatient with Krilon's slow, lengthy, rational speeches. Finally they expel him from the group. Deserted by his friends and faced with financial ruin, Krilon nonetheless battles on. He sends Hovall an eighteenth-century picture of the coronation of the Emperor of China, "the portly little emperor crowned in mildness by mild mandarins" (II, 350), in the hope that it will lead him away from Staph's more hectic and ruthless methods. Then ignoring his personal problems Krilon sets off on a journey to Norway to see how his old friends there are resisting German occupation and to present himself as a token of solidarity from an officially neutral Sweden. In traveling he leaves behind his woman friend, a Polish artist called Isabelle Verolyg. He promises to send her a message from Norway by carrier pigeon, but it never arrives, and in despair she commits suicide.

Krilon is deeply affected by the tragedy, yet he still manages to survive. The other members of the group, however, are now in a state of apathy, for they realize that by not sticking together under Krilon's leadership they have sold themselves to Staph, who has taken over their businesses. As Arpius puts it:

> I feel I'm like a surrounded, captured, occupied territory. It's the same with the whole group. Just now I no longer feel I'm *free,* at least not like before. Wasn't that what Krilon warned us about? Not letting them advance; not letting them advance from within us and not letting them advance from round about us. That's just what we did. The rumors, the whisperings, the attacks. We stepped aside and he stood there unprotected and couldn't protect us any longer. We fell, we crashed, the Devil got us. *But he's still there!*   (II, 276)

The others too begin to see their mistake. Hovall is deeply moved by the picture Krilon sends him. It inspires him to another of his visions, this time set in the graceful and mannered world of the eighteenth century, and there he understands what the picture means: "that one can lead men, lead great kingdoms, lead all humanity by slow, mild ceremonies" (II, 407).

Although Krilon's friends long to be rid of Staph they feel resistance is useless or impossible. The final blow comes when Krilon's office is set on fire and the police suspect Krilon of doing it himself to collect the insurance money. Krilon is forced to go into hiding. Minning, however, resolves to adopt a policy of active resistance to Staph, and turning detective he discovers that Staph is responsible for the fire and that he has an elaborate underground hideout in the cellars of the building. Krilon prepares for a counter-attack, in close consultation with an American colleague called Frank Lind and in less cordial alliance with Jekau, who is now under heavy fire from Staph. Krilon gathers his battered group together again, and this time they are able to talk about their problems, as they were not earlier. Eventually Krilon is able to lead them against Staph's hideout and in a furious brawl they rout Staph and his gang. Not, however, unscathed. Their businesses are in ruins; Krilon is badly hurt and is taken to hospital;

and poor Hovall, who has been delayed in a pub, comes late to the fray and is struck a fatal blow by the retreating forces. The last of his visions, of a trip to Heaven, becomes in a sense reality.

This is the basic story of the *Krilon* books. For all its comic and bizarre elements it is one of the most moving stories Johnson has written. Few of his characters are so sympathetically conceived and so well-rounded as the members of "Krilon's Group." Their various stories are really novels in themselves, and together they cover a wide sweep of human thought and emotion. Perhaps the finest of the characters, overshadowing even Krilon himself, is Hovall, with his human weaknesses but his gentle dreams of a better world: "We ought to be able to leave our ordinary lives and be other people and have other souls. I don't mean we've such bad souls now. But we ought to be different, at least sometimes" (II, 131). His longings are too delicate for the world he finds himself in. When he comes to Heaven he admits he is not altogether sorry to be "in a peace where I am not disturbed by life" (III, 594), and like another man whose soul is more beautiful than his body—Ceder in *Rain at Dawn*—he quotes the closing words of *The Winter's Tale*:

> Lead us from hence: where we may leisurely
> Each one demand, and answer to his part
> Perform'd in this wide gap of time, since first
> We were dissever'd: hastily lead away!

II   *The Interpretations*

The author declares in a personal appearance in the novel: "The story of this group is the story of a Swedish author's military service from January, 1941, up to now" (III, 682). This is the first aspect of the novel that must be considered. Krilon is actively engaged in what is happening in Europe. Indeed, one of the accusations the members of the group level at Krilon when they expel him is that he has not been neutral in the war between Germany and Britain. Krilon rejoins that he would consider it immoral if he were: "Being neutral can in certain cases mean standing calmly by watching a bull gore a child to death. I don't consider it useful for men to be neutral in such cases. I don't consider it useful for states either, but I don't want to drag that into the conversation. I am at war. I am on the side fighting for THE FREEDOM TO BE A HUMAN BEING, for the finest thing of all. The freedom to live at

peace. The freedom for every man to speak openly" (I, 534). Krilon
does not think that man and society are perfect as they are, but
without freedom they can never improve, and it is this freedom that
is threatened by the dictatorships in Europe. Development towards
better men, better societies, can only proceed via free discussion
and rational argument, not emotional intoxication and blind faith.
That is why Krilon feels that it is his war too, even if his government
declares otherwise, and that is why Krilon shows his solidarity
for the Norwegians in their resistance to the Germans.

The author uses Krilon as his mouthpiece and does not comment
directly on events. One of the major targets of the *Krilon* books is
the strange behavior of the Swedish government in its efforts to
preserve neutrality, yet it is attacked obliquely, through irony.
The main example of this occurs in the figure of Petrus Blarén,
a politician who represents the official policy of placating the
Germans and censoring embarrassing facts. Blarén's speeches
are masterpieces of evasion and contradiction. He recalls, for example, the speech in which he dealt with the delicate question of
German troop transports through Sweden: "In my speech I pointed
out that this friendly gesture towards a friendly power wasn't
induced by any kind of threat, and that anyway the trains in question
would run at night. But unfortunately my lips are sealed, I can't
go any deeper into the subject now" (III, 313). The portrait of
Blarén is so devastating that it is difficult not to sympathize with
his indignant cry: "Irony ought to be forbidden! . . . All opposition ought to be forbidden, I've always said so. What's the good
of democracy and fine responsible democratic policies if those
of us who are called to look after them can't be left in peace? So
that democracy can develop in peace *all opposition must be mercilessly stamped out!*" (III, 317–18).

While the *Krilon* trilogy is a contribution to the debate in Sweden
on the pros and cons of neutrality, it is also much more. Krilon,
the author explains, is "not a person in the usual sense; rather he
is an attempt at a figure, a draft of a figure, and his margins are
so wide that many lofty human thoughts and deep passions can
still be added" (I, 501). Krilon is not merely an estate agent with
business difficulties; he is also a character of allegorical and symbolic significance. His struggle with Staph is an allegory of events
in Europe, and ultimately it is the eternal struggle of Good against
Evil.

Firstly, the allegory. Krilon bears a strong physical resemblance to Churchill, and his role in the allegory is much that of Britain. His American friend Frank Lind is of course Franklin D. Roosevelt. The opposing forces are led by G. Staph: "His name was Staph with 'ph', but it was pronounced 'ph' and not 'f'" (I, 216), a pronunciation that emerges as Gestapo. He is assisted by a triumvirate called Görgöhö—Gören, Göbén, and Höllén—with the physical attributes and deformities of Goering, Goebbels, and Himmler. Staph's ally, and later his enemy, is T. Jekau, which suggests *tjeka,* the Swedish transcription of Stalin's secret police, "cheka." Names of other contemporary figures are disguised much as those of Goering and Goebbels—by their endings.

The contest between Krilon and Staph reflects that between Britain and Germany. At first Staph works with Jekau, just as Hitler was allied with Stalin. When Staph launches a business offensive against Jekau, analogous to Hitler's Russian campaign, Krilon reluctantly agrees to work with Jekau, as Churchill had worked with Stalin. The members of Krilon's group are compared to small European states. Krilon emphasizes again and again that they must stick together, for together they are a power, but divided they are defenseless and must fall one by one to the enemy. That is the significance of their search for Frid when he disappears: "Our position is not unlike that of a group of small states, where each of them must submit to inconveniences, even make sacrifices, for the sake of the others, so that the whole, the strength of the circle can be maintained if anything from outside threatens its independence. Even if the situation seems hopeless we must do our duty for the sake of a lofty principle" (I, 258–59). Krilon is striking particularly at the attitude of the Scandinavian governments who had not held together in the face of Russian aggression in the east, against Finland, and German occupation in the west, of Denmark and Norway. The group falls apart like Scandinavia; to repeat Arpius's words: "I feel I'm like a surrounded, captured, occupied territory." How the group fights back is compared to the resistance in German-occupied territory. Krilon says: "You must recognize, realize, establish the fact that you are like occupied states and that the only possibility of ending your misery is by fighting as best you are able. I have myself seen a people fighting almost without weapons, in darkness, at night, underground. You must try to be like the Norwegians" (III, 34–35). The group's struggle does in fact take place underground, in the cellars of Stockholm.

Sometimes the allegory operates in a rather too obvious way, such as when the Munich Agreement is described in a straight-forward one-to-one correspondence between statesmen and countries in Europe and businessmen and companies in the Stockholm real-estate market, but on the whole the "real" story of Krilon's group and its allegorical interpretation are subtly and impressively interwoven. An example is provided by the Atlantic Charter, which was signed on board a battleship by Churchill and Roosevelt. In *Krilon* Frank Lind and Krilon row out into Lake Mälaren in a rowboat "painted in the gray-blue color of a battleship" (III, 560) and produce their "Maelar Charter" (III, 559).

Krilon's role as Churchill is only one aspect of his extensive personality. At one point Krilon discusses the various names suggested by his initials JK (I, 542), but he ignores the obvious one: Jesus Kristus. He comes nearer to identifying himself with Christ when he talks to the group before his expulsion: "The members of the group were tried, and it was shown that they could not watch one hour, as it says in the New Testament . . . . Not that I want to compare myself to Christ or you to the disciples, as an anonymous person has suggested" (I, 532). The biblical parallels in the novel are as ingenious as the political. For example, Krilon is invited to lunch by Staph and Jekau in a restaurant at the top of a tall structure with a fine view of Stockholm, and there they try to persuade him to do a deal with them and divide up the world markets between them: "Krilon . . . was led up onto a fairly high mountain and tempted. The author . . . cannot, as things stand, assert that Krilon was tempted by the Devil, but is more and more inclined to think it was something of the sort" (I, 492). Hovall, in his strange meeting with Jekau-Staph, does see the enemy as the Devil with horns on his head, a toasting fork in his hand, and a general whiff of sulphur about him. When Krilon is expelled from the group, on Easter Sunday, the author writes that "Krilon was crucified" (II, 24). Krilon sends Hovall his picture of the Chinese coronation at Whitsuntide, a kind of parallel to the descending of the Holy Ghost. Krilon is even betrayed by one of his disciples, Odenarp playing Judas's role.

The intentions behind the references to Christ are rather different from those behind the political, contemporary comparisons. Krilon is not a stand-in for Christ in a religious allegory as he is for Britain in the political allegory. Rather, Christ and Krilon are

symbols of one idea: of Good in its struggle with Evil, of man's
attempt to develop his spiritual greatness in adversity. Krilon
summarizes his role as follows: "It's an eternal fight that I, a
humble person, have been granted the favor by life of continuing.
I am the simple servant of the Spirit" (II, 94). Like the struggle
against Staph, the struggle against evil is a fight against both
external and internal enemies. Every man can be overwhelmed
by evil forces acting within him and can then himself become a
force for evil in the world. These forces can break through when
men are thrown off balance by suffering or disappointment. The
fight against evil is largely a fight against the effects of despair and
disillusionment. An obvious example in the novel is provided by
Odenarp, who has tried to patent an invention, only to find that
a Jew has beaten him to it. In his deep disappointment he has
come to see all Jews as a menace and he is attracted to Nazism.
His tragedy is then compounded when he discovers his wife, and
so his children, have Jewish blood. A less schematic example of
the alternative course is Krilon, who has succeeded in overcoming
his grief and rage at losing his girl friend in the midsummer catastrophe and has used the tragedy to ennoble his life. Krilon discusses the significance of tragedy as follows:

There are people who after experiencing a great disappointment, or
something even worse—for there are worse things—or after merely suffering one setback are seized by a violent desire to assert themselves and assert themselves at all costs. People who deep down feel they
have failed and for that reason try to convince themselves and the world
that they aren't failures at all and that their life is guided by a mighty
fate, that they themselves have known this and felt like the chosen ones.
It's extensive, this subject. Haven't for example, dictators most often
arisen in this way?   (I, 70)

Tragedy also contains possibilities for good: "Above all, the
tragic experiences men have had have created a great deal of art.
That is an advantage" (I, 71). And art is an excellent weapon to
use against evil and disappointment, as Krilon well knows when
he sends his picture to Hovall: "It's like smuggling dynamite and
torpedoes and infernal machines into the enemy camp; the Emperor
of China is my fifth column" (II, 350). This is ultimately of course
the justification for the *Krilon* books and the author's description
of them as his military service. Clearly he shares Krilon's belief:

"I believe one can fight unhappiness and grief with genuine literature and music; yes, that one can fight the destructive forces now
with art, literature and music" (III, 488). Another source of consolation, as so often in Johnson's works, is nature. With Krilon,
as with Stormdal in *Commentary on a Falling Star,* it is oak trees
that provide relief from personal problems.

To summarize some of the interpretations that can be placed
upon the *Krilon* books, over and above the surface story of men
and their reactions to stress and disappointment: there is the
morality aspect, the concrete representation of man's fight against
the evil and destructive forces in life; there is the propaganda aspect
of the novel, in its direct engagement in the Second World War;
and there is its attempt to explain what exactly is happening, in
the simplified terms of an allegory. One particular episode that
illustrates much of all this, an independent short story within the
novel, is Krilon's meeting with the Buchmanite critic and journalist
Tollius. Tollius demands that Krilon should confess his sins, and
Krilon obliges with a confession of how he once killed an octopus
while fishing in a Norwegian fjord. The story is in one sense directly
polemical, an attack on one of Johnson's personal antagonists and
on Buchmanites in general. In another sense it is a lyrical hymn to
Scandinavia and its way of life. And the actual killing of the octopus,
when Krilon finally reaches it, has various connotations. It is a
gripping story of a man striking out in blind terror and panic at the
sight of an octopus. It is also a political symbol, the octopus representing "the secret police in dictatorships, a police organization
of the kind they have in the countries they have occupied" (II, 300),
a power stretching out its tentacles surreptitiously, in darkness.
The octopus has, too, a more spiritual symbolism: "A picture of
what is horrible in life or in the soul, rising from the depths, which
one feels one has to kill to be able to survive" (II, 288). It provokes
something similar in Krilon; he becomes a man who has to adopt
the weapons and nature of his enemy in his fight against it: "I was
a loathsome, panic-stricken figure doing battle with the weapons
of loathsomeness and fear against something loathsome" (II,
305). Krilon admits at the end that the story is untrue, for he did
not actually kill the octopus he saw in Norway, but the story is
not the less important for that: "It was my own fear I was trying
to describe to you, my own fear of what I saw then and what is
happening in the world and within men" (II, 308). The principles

behind Krilon's telling of this fairy tale—for such it is—lie behind the whole of the novel. It is now time to consider them.

III   *Narrative Technique*

Discussing his reasons for writing the *Krilon* series, Johnson claimed in a newspaper interview: "I wanted to give a comprehensive picture of the world as I myself saw it and in the form I like best, the novel."[2] To achieve this comprehensive picture he has employed his unrivaled ingenuity and technical inventiveness to the full, so that a proper study of the narrative techniques employed is well beyond the scope of this chapter. Here attention can merely be drawn to some of the individual features of the story: Hovall's dreams and visions, analogous to the fairy tales in *The Novel About Olof;* the speech in which Krilon deduces the characters of his friends from their names; the section in which Krilon's life story is told in terms of his collection of keys; or the exuberant parody of Secret Service logic in the adventures of Arble Jonasson-Språng, who is convinced Arpius is a dangerous agent. Only three aspects of the story can be considered in detail here: the exhaustive style; the author's role in the novel; and its "half-realistic" form.

The rather long-winded style Johnson adopts in the novel is, he indicates, a consequence of his aim of giving a comprehensive picture of things: "The whole thing is an attempt to describe a human being as thoroughly as possible. I don't know myself how far I have succeeded as far as that is concerned. And perhaps people merely think it's strange when, for example, I describe a face in six printed pages. But I wanted it to be exhaustive."[3] Here as an example is an extract from the section devoted to Krilon's nose:

Krilon's nose was elegantly classical, one of those rare noses that have not been destroyed or disjointed by Scandinavian colds, falls from scaffoldings, contemptuous wrinklings, nocturnal fights or alcoholic or moral depravity in connection with changing climates. It was a nose as straight as possible, just sufficiently angled, with a redness that came from health and not bacteria or drink; it was quite simply a nose with character, which followed the general style of his face and yet attained an even higher esthetic value.   (I, 16)

Such style obviously contains an element of self-irony, which prevents it from being purely art for art's sake, but it also has a

deeper ethical significance. Truth, the author seems to say, cannot
be reached by simplification but only by careful qualification and
discussion, by the use of the exact synonym. Krilon's way of speaking
is as laborious as his author's description of him, and he is contrasted with Staph, who adopts a dynamic but misleading and often
nonsensical brevity in his speech. Some critics see the influence of
Thomas Mann in the long descriptions of Krilon. Linder, for
example, claims Krilon is described "with an exhaustiveness and
in a formal style that Johnson has adopted from Thomas Mann's
novel about Joseph and his brothers."[4] Another critic has attempted
to trace Mann's wider influence on the story, particularly echoes
of *The Magic Mountain,* but the correspondences seem largely
superficial.[5]

Another interesting aspect of the novel is the role the author
adopts. Rather like Gide in *The Counterfeiters* the author of *Krilon*
is both the master and the servant of his characters, creating them
and yet being compelled to observe them as independent beings.
A similar ambiguity applies to the subject matter. Sometimes the
author seems compelled to record everything that comes his way,
every little detail in the characters' lives, every odd item in news
bulletins from the world around them, while at other times he
deliberately cuts his material to size, as when he announces that
Tollius must play a minor role in the novel, but if he develops
satisfactorily "he may be allowed to return" (II, 161). The author
is the servant of his story, "the re-narrator," with the following task:

> The re-narrator's role is to re-narrate, perhaps not exactly as he sees
> it, but so that what he sees can reach other people as pictures of what is
> real or likely, pictures of tendencies, instructions about the path he himself
> is groping his way along. In other words, he is not always the cook from
> whose oven and hands the finished, properly baked pie can be collected and
> carried out to the table. Often he is only the supplier of the raw material,
> which he himself has gotten in certain quantities from the great supplier of
> raw material—reality, dreams. His work can consist of handing it out,
> or handing out bits of it. In this way he can determine the high or low
> calorie and vitamin content and provide a recipe for its preparation, while
> the receiver, the reader, the person seeing it at second hand, can fry, boil,
> spice, and thicken it himself.   (II, 310–11)

Faced with the far-ranging and often contradictory reports on the
progress of the war, and with events that seem totally incredible,

the author has the right to be baffled by his story and leave it in incomplete form. He can attempt to convey his view of it all, determining the bias—the "vitamin content"—to some extent by selection and presentation, but he cannot present reality to the reader on a plate: "This is how I tell the story; in actual fact it's different, but you'd have to be different from me to be able to tell it any other way" (II, 311).

Why does the author tell the story the way he does? In his newspaper interview, Johnson stated: "Sometimes it is impossible to say what you mean in a realistic and comprehensible way. The *Krilon* series is half-realism. There is a consistent symbolism, but the people are genuine. Taken straight from reality." Within the novel Krilon himself discusses the problems of realism and fantasy. He considers the difficulty of describing the liquidation of the Jews in Poland and Lithuania. The participants themselves can scarcely describe it: "Of all the gigantic, horrible mass of reality there remain only fragments, figures, data, names of German executioners and places in Lithuania and Poland" (III, 522). These bare facts convey nothing to the reader. Somehow he must be made to re-experience the reality behind them, just as Tomas Gyllem in *Night Maneuvers* had to experience personal suffering to understand the reality behind Nazism. Such experience can be obtained through the mediation of art:

"If someone who has tried to re-experience such things in his soul can snatch a single living picture out of this compact block of suffering in a reality of executioners, then the whole reality appears before his eyes," Krilon said. "He can see it, he can reproduce it, convey it in a picture, in words that provoke a picture in us. By transforming, changing, compressing reality he can carry the truth about it further. Others, who have halted before the bloody horror of the figures, without grasping, without being able to believe that such things have happened only a few hundred miles from Sweden can come to know through the mediation of this story, this re-creation, *what it was really like!* And it's this—what really happened— that he must strive to tell." (III, 523)

This is what Johnson has attempted to do in *Krilon*. He has tried to present the issues and events in more immediate, human terms, as the fates of members of a group, their businesses, and their enemies. Yet the nature of what he is describing is so fantastic that he cannot do more than guess at what is happening: "The cellar vaults of older literature, where there is both terror and fascination, have stepped out of literature into reality," Krilon observes (III, 341). Consequently, the novel cannot be more than what its subtitle suggests: "A Novel about the Probable." And faced with a reality even grimmer than that in *The Novel About Olof,* the author is again forced to resort to the fairy tale: "The writer often flees to the fairy tale to be able to describe reality, and sometimes to reality to bring out the cruel or beautiful meaning behind the fairy tale. Reality often hits out at us: we dodge it as best we can. One way is to close our eyes; another is to disguise it" (III, 521). Johnson could not close his eyes; *Krilon* is his form of disguise.

CHAPTER 6

A Subtler Sphinx

I Introduction

JOHNSON'S early interest in classical Greek literature has already been mentioned; this interest finds literary expression from the very beginning in his works in the title of "Joiner-Professor Tantalus" in *The Four Strangers* (1924).[1] Homer, with the *Odyssey,* and Xenophon, with his *Anabasis,* are the Greek authors that appear to be his favorites, and references to their works appear in several of Johnson's novels. In *Remembering* Mr. Clerk is compared to Odysseus, Mrs. Berr to Nausicaa, and Ivar to Telemachus (161–62). In *Commentary on a Falling Star* the *Odyssey* is appealed to for the purposes of illustration: "Beginnings, the mighty beginnings that never lead to anything, that are halted by a whim, by chance. When Ulysses came ashore, his legs folded under him, the song says" (277). A similar use of the *Anabasis* occurs in *Rain at Dawn,* when Henrik Fax and Affe stare towards Karin's house: "In the same way the returning warriors in the *Anabasis* sat on high mountains and stared in the direction in which they thought Greece lay" (117). In *Farewell to Hamlet* it is one of the characters and not the author who uses Xenophon to provide an example, when Mårten Torpare refers to the peculiar moral code of the Mossynoici (*Anabasis,* V, 4)[2] in talking about civilization (110ff.). The most extended use of the *Anabasis* in this way is by Krilon in *Krilon Himself,* when he talks about the book as "in many ways a perfect classical tragedy" (519) which he puts into modern dress so that the members of his group can understand the reality behind it.

To refer to Homer and Xenophon in this way seems natural to Johnson, for literary and personal experiences are not essentially different for him; literature and life are inseparable. Olof, for example, in *Finale in Youth,* thinks of the soldiers in the *Anabasis* when he tramps through the snow on his way to work. Homer and Xenophon are not just authors who provide useful parallels now and then. They are an integral part of Johnson's and his characters' consciousness.

Johnson's first attempts to write about Ancient Greece are in short-story form, four such stories being published in *The Night Has Come* (1932). In these stories Johnson presents his characters in a rather ridiculous light, relying for comic effect on the contrast between Greece as it is usually conceived—romantically and heroically—and the more primitive society he describes. One of the stories is an unheroic account of Homer's life, "En man från Etolien" ("A Man from Aetolia"), presumably referring to the scoundrel mentioned by Eumaeus in the *Odyssey* (Book XIV). In another story, "Kimon," Johnson pokes fun at Greek philosophy, playing with both Heraclitus's notion that everything is in a state of flux and Zeno's paradoxes that prove that nothing ever moves. Kimon sits motionless with an equally motionless tortoise in the village square demonstrating the impossibility of motion—until his tortoise suddenly flies away. But entertaining though these stories are, Johnson's most important works concerned with Ancient Greece are two novels: *Strändernas svall* (*The Swell on the Beaches,* 1946) and *Molnen över Metapontion* (*The Clouds over Metapontion,* 1957).

II *A New Ulysses*

The Swell on the Beaches (tr. as *Return to Ithaca*) is a retelling of the *Odyssey,* with nearly, but not quite, the same story as the original. The following is the plot of Johnson's version: Nineteen years before the story begins, Odysseus, ruler of the island of Ithaca, has reluctantly left his wife Penelope and baby son Telemachus to join the Greek forces in their attack on Troy. The war has lasted ten years, and on his way home Odysseus has been diverted and delayed by various disasters until finally he has come to the remote island where a woman called Calypso lives. He is now in his seventh year on the island, unwilling or unable to return home. On Ithaca Penelope hesitates to remarry though it appears she must now be a widow. She is pestered by a large number of suitors, who sponge on her hospitality and threaten to eat her into financial ruin. She delays them by saying that she cannot make a decision until she has woven a winding-sheet for her supposedly ailing father. She weaves by day but undoes most of her weaving at night. The story is set in motion by Hermes, messenger of the gods, who visits Odysseus and orders him to return home. Reluctantly Odysseus sets off on a raft towards Ithaca. Meanwhile Telemachus, now a young man, has been encouraged to look for his father and he travels in search of information to his father's old comrades-in-arms, Nestor and Menelaus. Odysseus is wrecked in a storm and cast ashore on a coast ruled by King Alcinous of the Phaeacians. It is Alcinous's young daughter Nausicaa who discovers Odysseus and takes him to court. Odysseus wins over the Phaeacians by a gripping recital of his adventures since the sack of Troy, and they ferry him home to Ithaca. He comes disguised as a beggar to the hut of his faithful swineherd Eumaeus. Odysseus has no desire to get involved in further bloodshed, but Eumaeus insists he deal with the suitors. With the help of Telemachus and Eumaeus Odysseus then organizes the mass murder of his wife's suitors and their mistresses and children.

From a summary of the plot Odysseus might appear to be a warlike and bloodthirsty character, but in fact he becomes a soldier in spite of himself. When Agamemnon and Menelaus came to "persuade" him to join their expedition against Troy, he pretended to be mad, plowing with an ox and ass and sowing salt. He had no desire to go to war: "Perhaps I was more a farmer than a prince or seaman or warrior" (53). But he realized that if he did not accompany the Greek chieftains they would destroy Ithaca. Paradoxically, the only way to stay secure at home was to make the journey via Troy; he sacrificed Troy to save Ithaca. But it has proved difficult to return home from Troy. The bloodshed and brutality of war have sickened him. He thinks of the slaves casually sacrificed in battle, of his comrades lost on the homeward voyage, but most of all he is tortured by the memory of Astyanax, the child heir to the Trojan throne, dashed to death on Odysseus's advice. Anxious to escape these memories, Odysseus finds welcome refuge with Calypso on her island, isolated from the world.

Calypso's whole being is eroticism; her demands are insatiable. Odysseus is ensnared by her charms, but creeps into her bed "with reluctance and pleasure, with disgust and desire" (11). He is captured by his own desires and her ability and skill as a partner: "It's the binding experience of middle age. I am a prisoner in that combination of blood and spirit" (13). Yet although Odysseus is a willing captive on Calypso's island, he does not find the relief

he seeks. He can only repress his memories, not destroy them.
The boy he killed at Troy and the son he left at home lie just below
the surface of his thoughts. Moreover, time passes, however much
he pretends not to count the days. Minutes fall like drops of water
into a water tub and eventually the tub must overflow. At the beginning of the novel the point of overflow appears to have been reached.
Watching the swell on the beaches Odysseus meditates on his
position and directs an anguished plea to Zeus to help him:
"I can stand everything, but not the thought that the years slip by,
that time exists, that lives can be changed without my being there—
now" (19).

The arrival of Hermes with the gods' command that Odysseus
must leave decides the issue. When Odysseus sees Hermes he
realizes that time has caught up with him: "They could hear the
sea, the swell washing on both the beaches. 'The years,' he thought.
'Now they are rolling over me.' " (25). Even then Odysseus cannot
make the final decision himself. He refuses to accept Hermes's
offer of a boat and leaves the onus of providing transport to Calypso.
In effect she has to throw him out. Yet when he has broken up from
Calypso he does not allow himself to be diverted from a journey he
scarcely wishes to make. When he is shipwrecked among the Phaeacians and is offered the hand of Nausicaa in marriage he does not
accept, but does his best to get the Phaeacians to ferry him home
by telling them stories: "He fought with words, nuances, gestures,
for the completion of his own fate, for his journey home to the
unknown. He was driven by his inner haste towards goals which
in fact he did not want to attain" (420). Why then is Odysseus so
reluctant to leave Calypso for his native shore, and why does he
finally do so?

Odysseus discusses the question in terms of gods and divine
commandments. He believes that man's fate is controlled by the
gods. On his perilous raft he makes suitable genuflections to the
Pantheon, just to be on the safe side, but his real attitude is one of
hostility. He criticizes the gods for their largely neutral stance
during the Trojan War, and Hermes himself confirms that the gods
do not want to get *too* involved in Odysseus's affairs: "We cannot
undertake to support an uprising, if his return should be regarded
as an attempt at an uprising against the party that has a large share
of the power on Ithaca" (89). The gods set things in motion, but
they are largely indifferent to the results or the human suffering

involved. Odysseus feels that human experience speaks against the gods' decrees. He puts his thoughts hesitantly and ingeniously to Calypso:

"Every time I sense an order from them, the gods, I also sense that I am acting wrongly in obeying it. Yet it's all we can do. But we can ask ourselves: How do they guide the world? The question is free, they themselves have placed its possibility in my breast. But I am punished if I answer it."

"If you answer wrongly," she said.

"We always answer wrongly if we take the truth for the answer from our own experience, Calypso. . . . *If* Zeus has placed thoughts in my skull, they are *his* thoughts. But he hasn't placed thoughts in my head, only the possibilities of thought. He has given me an instrument. I can play what I can play, no more. Or I can put it like this: He has given me a jigsaw puzzle. It can give rise to many shapes, but none outside the possibilities of the puzzle. We can say: The man who made the puzzle is responsible for its possibilities. . . . With my experiences and my unfathomable ignorance, my dark blindness, I should guide the world differently. Obviously, differently. Who could guide it like the Almighty?" (113–15)

Odysseus knows what the gods have decreed. The goals for which he must leave Calypso and ignore Nausicaa are clear: "His tragic fate to be a divine instrument of Justice, to be The Executioner" (418). Justice, abstract, divine justice, demands Odysseus's return to his wife and the destruction of the suitors who have usurped his palace and island. Odysseus's human experience, however, tells him that killing must be avoided at all costs. He tells Hermes that he does not want to go to war again. He senses dimly that there must be an alternative: "I can say that it is a defensive war, but all the same it isn't the truth. Far in the east, at the end of the world, among the barbarians living there, they have other, correct expressions for it, but I can't find them" (63).

Eumaeus, the swineherd Odysseus meets on his return home, suggests an alternative way of looking at the problem. He discusses what Odysseus might do if he were to return home, well knowing that the beggar before him is Odysseus. There are, Eumaeus claims, two different reasons for executing the suitors. One is the argument Odysseus is familiar with: that the gods demand it. It then becomes a question of power; power changes hands, from the suitors to Odysseus, who from a theoretical point of view has more "right" to wield it. But such divine bookkeeping has little to do with man's happiness. Eumaeus says of the gods' rule: "Their power is a wagon rolling of its own accord and crushing anything lying in the way— playfully" (483). Odysseus agrees that divine decrees have little relevance to human feelings, but since they stand behind everything we cannot ignore them. Eumaeus is not sure:

> "Sometimes I've thought that there is something behind the gods," Eumaeus said. "*You and me*. Masters and slaves, old and young. *Men*. Perhaps the gods were created many thousands of years ago, in a barbaric past, a confused and anxious age which wasn't at all like our civilized age here on Ithaca and the mainland . . . . Perhaps the gods were created then, born in men's breasts. It's a thought almost impossible to think. We don't really understand it because now we're in the hands of the gods, under their will. But just suppose the hands of the gods withered? That we had a will of our own? Then we'd fall out of their hands. Then only men would be left. And then we would have to save the situation ourselves, and we would do it because we should realize how serious it was."   (481)

Eumaeus's argument seems to be that the gods and the code of behavior they represent belong to an earlier stage in human development, when society was organized on the basis of an eye for an eye, a tooth for a tooth. Man creates gods as symbols of his ethical principles; but his symbols, from being an aid to his understanding of the world, become his prisoners. His mind is shackled by the concepts of his ancestors, though they may bear little relation to his own society and civilization.

Eumaeus thinks it wrong that Odysseus should proceed against the suitors merely from traditional reasons of "justice" and "revenge." But he suggests another reason for his taking action. The suitors are only interested in their own power. They are leading Ithaca towards slavery and dictatorship. Odysseus can destroy their tyranny, not to replace it with his own but to provide the possibilities of a better, more human society. His execution of the suitors is brutal butchery, Eumaeus leaves him in no doubt about that, and the result can only provide "a point of departure" (484) for something better. What will happen then is vague; Eumaeus can only guess what men may do when they liberate themselves from divine concepts and learn from earthly experience: "Perhaps then they will divide up power. Perhaps then they won't have slaves. Perhaps then they will hold discussions instead of making war, will trade instead of plundering. Perhaps then they will share their bread equally. But it's so distant. I can't see it clearly. I do not see a goal, only a direction. In a thousand or two thousand or three thousand years perhaps the Kingdom of Man will come" (483–84).

Odysseus has two arguments to choose between: he can kill the suitors because it is the customary thing to do, or he can set out on a new course and kill the suitors to create a new sort of society. It is not altogether clear which reason he finally adopts; indeed, he proceeds rather like a sleepwalker to the final reckoning. He seems to place himself at the gods' disposal: "He was not a human being, nor was he a god; he was only a human body in the power of the sportive gods. He was War within these four walls, a man poisoned by war, inflamed by Ares" (593–94). Perhaps he cannot in the end escape the gods and the power they wield over his thoughts. And whatever the reason for his acting, the outcome must be disastrous. His action will provoke reaction as far as man can see: "The stone he hurls into the sea will produce a swell not only against this coast. It will produce a swell against all beaches. Everything is connected. . . . The swell from Ithaca will reach every man in every age, in all ages after us" (486–87).

Odysseus is only too well aware of his tragic fate. In a dream he projects his knowledge into an interview with the seer Teiresias in the Underworld. The seer tells him:

You will lose all your comrades and become the loneliest man on earth. Your journey will continue for ever. You must travel deep into yourself against your will. You must drink up drop by drop all the blood of men and children that you have spilt, and you won't like the taste. All the bodies you have opened with lance and sword and arrow and knife and club and stone will pour their blood over you. It will burn you, son of Ares. You will hide in women's embraces and in the embraces of stories and lies, and when you've forgotten everything a message will rise from within you and a message will come from outside with the memory of it all. You will be called home when you no longer want to go home. That will be your fate.(199)

Eventually he may achieve happiness, when he exchanges war for agriculture, as he had wanted to before leaving for Troy. He must take an oar and head inland:

If you then meet a man who asks you if it's a spade you're carrying over your shoulder you should answer yes and begin digging in the ground with the oar. Then perhaps you will find happiness, perhaps happiness

is buried in that very spot. Then perhaps you will emerge from your loneliness to meet beings who dig in the ground with simple spades for happiness and who don't dig for happiness with sword and lance in other men's
bodies. Then perhaps you will be a completely new man, the very first
of a new sort.   (200)

Those familiar with Homer will realize that while the events of
The Swell on the Beaches closely resemble those of the *Odyssey,* the
problems discussed in Johnson's novel are completely alien to the
spirit of the epic poem. It is instructive to consider Johnson's work
in comparison with Homer's.

The *Odyssey* is a work of fantasy, a tall story, whereas Johnson
has tried to provide in *The Swell on the Beaches* a realistic interpretation of events, on the assumption that Odysseus's journey really
did take place. His sources are first and foremost the *Odyssey,*
but he has also used more scientific and historical works on the
subject, in particular Victor Bérard's commentary to the *Odyssey.*[3]
Johnson's realistic approach to the subject compels him to make
the characters more human and less heroic and to make the fantastic
events that befall them more credible.[4]

Firstly, the characterization. Johnson has either seized on traits
inherent in Homer's characters, though not necessarily developed
in the poem, or reinterpreted events to throw a different light on
the characters. The three members of Odysseus's family—Odysseus,
Penelope, and Telemachus—are treated in this way. Homer's
Odysseus is anxious to escape Calypso and deal with the suitors.
Johnson, however, seizes on Odysseus's seven years with Calypso
and his self-control in waiting for the right moment to destroy
the suitors when he arrives on Ithaca, and he puts a different interpretation on them. Perhaps Odysseus does not want to leave
Calypso, perhaps he does not want to kill the suitors. Homer's
Odysseus is untroubled by the rights and wrongs of war and by
his murder of Astyanax, but how could a normal man nowadays
not be affected by pangs of conscience? Homer's hero is also insen-
sitive to the passing of time, while Johnson's Odysseus is haunted
by the thought that after twenty years he is changed, and no one
will recognize him when he comes home: "Perhaps they will recognize my body and call me by my name. But they will never recognize
me" (509–10).

Just as Odysseus becomes burdened with the human failings of indecision, guilt, and aging, so too his wife becomes more fallible and human in her modern reappearance. In the *Odyssey* she is utterly faithful to Odysseus, but indecisive in relation to the suitors, neither accepting nor rejecting them. Johnson has seized on this trait to doubt her fidelity, for perhaps twenty years' fidelity is a lot to demand in the twentieth century. Penelope is a middle-aged woman, plucking out her first grey hairs, and she has a woman's desires: "What had Penelope in the sixteenth year, at the beginning of the suitors' reign, once given Antinous, young, strong, energetic? Was it more than the touching of lips? . . . Who knows what a half-widow, wife of a husband on a long journey, feels in her body when the invigorating scents of the year are in the air and there is the smell of virile, fully potent youth in the vicinity?" (92). She hesitates between her wish to be faithful to Odysseus and her desire to have a young husband in her bed, and her actions reflect the superiority of now one, now the other feeling. She is scarcely pleased when Odysseus returns, an old man, "a war-ruined wreck" (593).

Telemachus, her son, is diffident compared with his father in the *Odyssey,* and Johnson increases his diffidence in *The Swell on the Beaches.* He is an honest and straightforward character who despises his mother's stratagems for delaying her remarriage; he cannot understand her lack of logic in both striving for it and rejecting it. Odysseus prophesies of him: "That man will possibly be a pretty sensible, but perhaps not markedly wise or clear-sighted ruler, a good-natured but perhaps slightly stolid king" (504).

Two characters who play a minor role in the *Odyssey* are elevated to more important positions in *The Swell on the Beaches.* The swineherd Eumaeus acts as the raisonneur of the novel, while Odysseus's old nurse, Eurycleia, is in effect Penelope's chief adviser and executive. She pretends to be more or less deaf and hopelessly short-sighted, which restricts her to hearing and seeing what she wants to. Her health is allegedly delicate, and she goes on long journeys to springs and spas, journeys which result in vast economic transactions between Ithaca and other states. Yet in front of Penelope she plays a subordinate role, proffering advice only in roundabout ways, such as by narrating her always highly relevant dreams. Her delightful and hilarious activities are Johnson's invention and lack any basis in Homer. While Eumaeus and Eurycleia are promoted by Johnson, he can reduce heroic characters from the *Odyssey* almost to caricatures. Nestor becomes a doddering, though lovable, old man; Menelaus and Helen are a sentimental old couple with a fondness for drink, Helen herself being plump and rather too heavily made up; and Teiresias, the noble prophet, is a rheumatic and querulous old gentleman.

Characterization provides one obvious difference between Homer and Johnson; the arrangement of the story provides another. Johnson has reorganized the sequence of events of the *Odyssey* and altered the balance between the different episodes. *The Swell on the Beaches* is more involved, plots being interwoven in a less clear-cut manner than in the *Odyssey*. The *Odyssey* begins with a brief introduction to the existing state of affairs, continues with Telemachus's journey to Nestor and Menelaus, then switches to Odysseus's journey from Calypso and his stay among the Phaeacians. Speaking to the Phaeacians Odysseus recapitulates his journey from Troy to Calypso's island. The second half of the *Odyssey* then deals straightforwardly with Odysseus's actions on Ithaca. Johnson has rearranged the first half by interweaving Odysseus's actions with those of Penelope and Telemachus. The first five-eighths of the book devotes chapters alternately to Odysseus, alternately to Penelope and Telemachus. The themes run parallel: Odysseus hesitates over Calypso, but is forced to leave; Penelope resists the suitors, but is made to name the day; Odysseus's journey home is contrasted with Telemachus's search for him, and when Odysseus meets and ignores Nausicaa, his son meets and falls in love with Nestor's daughter.

Further, Odysseus's adventures between leaving Troy and coming to Calypso, narrated *en bloc* in the *Odyssey,* are spread out in *The Swell on the Beaches*. Some is told to Calypso, some comes as dreams, some finally is told to the Phaeacians; for memory to Johnson is not something that can be served up as required and otherwise ignored—it comes involuntarily. Apart from reorganizing events in this way Johnson has also altered the balance in his novel to give a much fuller version than Homer of the earlier part. While half the *Odyssey* is devoted to Odysseus on Ithaca, only about a quarter of *The Swell on the Beaches* deals with these events. In compensation, the relationships between Odysseus and Calypso, and Penelope and Eurycleia and the suitors are more deeply explored in Johnson's novel. *The Swell on the Beaches* ends with Odysseus's killing of the suitors, while the *Odyssey* continues with the ensuing feud between Odysseus and the suitors' avengers and with Pallas Athene's

final intervention to put an end to it. Of course there can be no such
end in *The Swell on the Beaches:* the waves of blood will never be
stilled.

By the above means Johnson creates a story which is more psychological and philosophical in its emphasis than Homer's tale
of adventure. Yet there are obvious difficulties in incorporating
some episodes from the *Odyssey* into a realistic novel. The *Odyssey*
is happily acted out in a world of nymphs, sea monsters, one-eyed
giants, gods and goddesses. How has Johnson reduced this to realistic terms?

Sometimes features of the *Odyssey* are adapted without comment.
For example, Homer's Odysseus is saved from drowning by a
veil given him by the goddess Ino in the guise of a seabird, while
Johnson's Odysseus receives a life belt of cork from Calypso, given
her, she claims, by a nymph called Ino (145). Often, however,
divergences from Homer are discussed in the text. When Odysseus
faces his son for the first time for twenty years, Homer lets Pallas
Athene transform Odysseus into a suitably impressive father.
Johnson writes of the episode: "The change which occurred here has,
like much else, been attributed to Pallas Athene. But it was not a
display of magic. It was a fully acceptable—though perhaps
unusual—changing of clothes" (505). Homer is more directly
criticized over the number of suitors Odysseus is supposed to have
killed: "And, the song says, there were many more. But that must
be an exaggeration. No human minstrel, not even the gods, can
arrange and fulfill the fates of a hundred and eight or fifty-two people
in such a small room, with a quiver containing only forty arrows"
(567). Occasionally Homer is dismissed out of hand. On the Phaeacians' return from ferrying Odysseus to Ithaca: "In the thirteenth
book of the *Odyssey* we can, if we wish, read that the returning
Phaeacians' ship was turned to an island rock" (461). Johnson's
treatment of the gods and goddesses in the story is, however, a
little ambiguous. Calypso is treated as though she really had eternal
life. Hermes appears in person at the beginning of the novel, but
the solidity of his substance is unclear. When Odysseus is asked why
he left Calypso: " 'I got a message,' he said. 'It was an inner call.
No, it was Hermes' " (457). Teiresias also emphasizes in the speech
reproduced above that the call to Odysseus is an inner call as well
as a call from outside. It is tempting to believe that in this case a
god is being used as a concrete projection of an abstract thought,

very much as Eumaeus wonders if the gods are not ultimately man's expression for his own tenets.

The most extensive and important reinterpretation of Homer occurs in Odysseus's account of his adventures after the fall of Troy. Like Krilon, Johnson's Odysseus realizes that a fantastic, fairy-tale treatment of events can often make them more comprehensible to people than a strictly realistic account. This he demonstrates when he entertains the Phaeacians: "Here on the Phaeacians' island of Scheria he gathered up reality in his hands, the cruel, crude reality of the outside world, the mountains, the seas, and broke it up into crumbs and scattered it in fragments as fairy tales, sowed it like glittering corn" (418). When Circe's wine turns Odysseus's men into pigs, as it does in the *Odyssey,* Johnson's Odysseus is well aware that it is the men's drunken behavior, rather than their bodies, that can be called swinish. Odysseus's personal feud with Poseidon is only a dramatic representation of his struggles with the sea. His visit to Hades, "The Kingdom of Hopelessness," is a way of describing his extreme depression. A good example of Odysseus's technique is the story of his encounter with the cyclops Polyphemus:

[The Phaeacians'] expectancy and belief carried him away from the reality he had experienced for ten or twenty years to the reality they wanted the warrior with the famous name to have experienced. He could have said that he had landed on volcanic islands or coasts broken up by volcanic eruptions, where extinct or dormant craters stared up at the sky like cyclops' eyes, and where the living and active volcanoes hurled rocks at him and his men. The listeners wouldn't have believed him then. But when he said the fire-breathing mountains were gods with torches in their hands and the rocks were not slung up out of the craters but hurled by giant hands, then they were ready to believe him and pass the story on.   (419)

There is reality behind the fantastic stories Odysseus tells, but he disguises it in the interests of realism. A further example may indicate the efficacy of this technique. Nestor tells Telemachus about Troy: "We knocked together something like storming ladders and a wooden horse—well, a kind of horse, some scaffolding that looked like a horse and which we called 'The Horse'; some clambered over the walls and opened the gates for us" (279). The concept of the Trojan Horse clearly makes a much greater appeal to the imagination and the memory than ordinary scaffolding.

The style of *The Swell on the Beaches* is circuitous, both in language and thought. The author himself indicates his leisurely, roundabout approach when he presents alternative ways of describing one scene—a slave girl crossing the courtyard of Penelope's house (37–39). First he describes the scene in a clipped, hard-boiled style, but then he adds: "Yes, truth, told directly, powerfully reproduced, might appear like that. But it can also be told another way" (38–39). The alternative way proves to be a lengthy and careful description of the courtyard and an exhaustive examination of the girl's thoughts. Johnson believes that nuances are vital, and his descriptions must be involved so that nothing is lost. Considerable space at the beginning of the novel is devoted to Odysseus's mouth, and small oral details lead to far-reaching conclusions about Odysseus's character and life history. Johnson seldom uses a simple expression if a more complicated one is available. The sun is not the sun but "the sympathetic and cruel Helios, one of the gods' spies, with other names in barbaric states and human settlements" (5). Odysseus is very rarely referred to by name; instead Johnson adopts Homer's device of epithets: "The Husband, The Traveler, The Man Longed for in This House and possibly Feared" (37). Sometimes the author seems to mock his own extravagances: for example, when he talks about spreading out a cloth in the sun: "As it is called in a rather elevated way—to give it Helios's unshadowed whiteness; or otherwise—to bleach it" (165). The dialogue too is often conducted in extravagantly long and elegant speeches.

The circuitousness in language is intimately connected with a circuitous approach to the subject matter. The author presents himself as a cautious historian, "the re-narrator" or "the guesser, the assumer, the latter-day searcher for motifs" (186). The author approaches his story obliquely, with guesses and assumptions rather than categorical statements. Is Penelope faithful? Possibly, possibly not. And the winding-sheet—how could she spend three years on it without arousing the suitors' suspicions? "Naturally they found her out. It was the third year from the beginning of the sheet. The latter-day re-narrator, who kneels beneath the weight of the narrative and so sees it somewhat from underneath, is inclined to think they found her out earlier and guessed the circumstances" (183). Where the facts are incredible the author must find likely explanations; he cannot make unqualified assertions. That is why he resorts to a vague, noncommittal style. On the other hand he can also show his regard for the truth by a scholarly exactitude when such is possible. He calculates the quantity of food that the suitors must have consumed (80–82) and the length of time it would really have taken Penelope to weave the winding-sheet (185). He can even give a gratuitous display of pedantry when the rambling Nestor stumbles on the place name Tenedos: "Tenedos was a key word, and when the old man pronounced it he got caught in another word which had nothing to do with the island but with *tendos*, 'gourmet,' (and the old man smacked his lips), or perhaps 'wasps' nest,' *tendrenion*" (299).

Language and thought are inseparable in these stylistic devices, and this is even more true of perhaps the most noticeable trait in Johnson's works: irony. It is both a stylistic device and an attitude to life, often a defense against over-violent emotion. When Odysseus leaves Calypso, she says: "You can do what you like with me. You can have me punished for being a fool, if you stay. You can break my heart if you do me the service of leaving me' 'Those are such lofty words,' he replied with irony" (113). Odysseus disguises his feelings as he has disguised his appearance when he meets Penelope for the first time for twenty years:

"Our guest, our highly honored guest, wants a footbath," Penelope said. "He thinks his feet smell."

"My lady, you use such mild words." he said. "I think my feet stink. I cannot understand how you, my lady, can put up with the stink of my aged feet."

"My husband, my late husband, used to employ that way of speaking," she said. "He had such funny expressions sometimes, he could be so cunning and witty in his speech, so exaggeratedly, ironically humble, so abrupt." (551–52)

Like *Krilon, The Swell on the Beaches* is a novel that can be appreciated on several planes. Firstly, it is an adventure story in a historical setting, with a devious, teasing style. Secondly, it invites an inevitable comparison with the *Odyssey* with all that it entails in the way of recognizing the similarities and differences. Thirdly, *The Swell on the Beaches* is a discussion of the problems facing men in the Second World War: its subtitle is "A Novel About the Present." The arguments that Eumaeus presents about the use of force in destroying tyranny are equally relevant to twentieth-century Europeans as to Odysseus. The forces on Ithaca bear a strange resemblance to those in Europe in 1940. Eumaeus declares: "There is a group of suitors from Same who dream of being lords of the whole world if only they can get power on the island. There is another group, from this island, who say they want power to govern for the people. They say that they will rule the island, or the world, for the good of the people. But they want to govern themselves" (485). The first group sound rather like Nazis in their ambitions, while the second suggest they have a lot in common with the founders of "People's Democracies."

Odysseus, like Krilon, is ultimately a symbol of Man. As he says on Calypso's isle: "Anthropos is my new name. . . . Damned Anthropos" (14). He is man at the mercy of a cruel universe and powers indifferent to his fate. In a dramatic illustration of his position there is the scene when he is caught in a storm, buffeted by forces beyond his control, pincered on his raft between the powers of heaven and water. He can only echo the cry he utters in the fifth book of the *Odyssey:* "In his language, in his mumbled dialect, he shaped words that contained the pride that comes from fear and that his greatest praisers, those who came nearest to him and saw him most clearly, translated as *Omoi ego!,* 'Poor Wretch!'" (246–47).

III *A Perfect Tragedy*

Xenophon's *Anabasis* is the account of the Hellenic troops who assisted Cyrus in his campaign against his brother Artaxerxes for possession of the Persian Empire. Together with Cyrus's forces they marched into Asia, to the frontiers of Babylon, and there they engaged Artaxerxes' army at the Battle of Cunaxa (401 B.C.). The Hellenes won a convincing victory on their wing, only to find Cyrus slain elsewhere on the field. Since their campaign was now meaningless they were forced to retreat and fight their way back through hostile and strange country, over the mountains of Armenia, to the Black Sea.

Johnson deals very differently with the *Anabasis* from the *Odyssey* when he comes to retell it in *The Clouds over Metapontion.* He follows the career of a member of the Persian expedition, Themistogenes, but grants him only half a novel. The other half is concerned with a journey to Italy undertaken by a twentieth-century Swede, Klemens Decorbie. The two stories will first be considered on their own, and then the methods by which they are combined into one novel will be investigated.

Klemens Decorbie, born in 1909, a Swede of Walloon descent,

marries an Irish girl called Cora and has two children by her.
At the beginning of the Second World War he enlists as a volunteer
in the French Army and is taken prisoner by the Germans; his wife
and children escape to England. In the prisoner-of-war camp he
meets a Jewish archeologist, Jean-Pierre Lévy, who entertains the
prisoners by describing the adventures of one Themistogenes of
Athens and Syracuse, a boyhood friend of Xenophon. Klemens
promises Lévy that he will visit Themistogenes' old haunts at
Metapontion (present-day Metaponto, Italy) when the war is over.
Lévy disappears, presumably into the gas ovens, but Klemens
finally comes to a labor camp in East Prussia. There he meets a
French girl, Claire Feltesse, also a prisoner, and he tries to seduce
her; but he discovers he is impotent. Afterwards he escapes to
Sweden, and Cora and the children set sail from England to join
him. Their boat is torpedoed and they are drowned. When the book
begins, ten years after the war, Klemens is working as a writer and
as an assistant to the European Refugee Commission. The story
starts by his flying from Stockholm to London. He has several ob-
jectives in mind: to honor his promise to Lévy and visit Metaponto;
to look for Claire and consummate his uncompleted relationship
with her; and to improve his finances, particularly by writing an
adventure book. From London he continues to Paris, where he
meets Jean-Pierre Lévy's widow and receives from her the manuscript of the projected work on Themistogenes. Klemens then travels
south through Italy. In Rimini he suddenly sees Claire, together
with a corpulent man he recognizes as one of her former guards
in Prussia. Klemens finally comes to Metaponto and visits the
temple ruins—all that survives of the former Greek colony where
Themistogenes once lived. Here again he meets Claire and the
German, who is called Heinz and is a traveling salesman. Klemens
stays some time in Metaponto, until on a day trip to Taranto he
meets Claire, appearing as a singer at a charity fete. Her next
engagement is in Syracuse, Sicily, and Klemens decides to accompany her there. She reveals that she is pregnant, a fact that has led
to Heinz's disappearance. While whispering words of endearment
to Klemens, she has her attention elsewhere and during the journey
to Syracuse keeps looking for Heinz. Eventually she discovers
him in Syracuse and leaves Klemens. When Klemens visits the
old stone quarries in Syracuse, where Themistogenes had once been
imprisoned, he sees Claire and Heinz and tries to make contact

with them, but they run away from him. Later, on his way back to Sweden, he reads that they have fallen—or thrown themselves—to their deaths in the quarries.

The other major character in the novel, Themistogenes, born about 435 B.C. in Athens, comes to Sicily on Alcibiades' ill-fated expedition (413 B.C.) and is taken prisoner. He is set to work in the stone quarries in Syracuse, but he wins the Sicilian tyrant's favor by his literary gifts and is released. He establishes himself with his wife and two children as an advocate in Syracuse. However, in some way he annoys the ruler, who engineers the death of his wife and two children and then places all kinds of obstacles in his path. Penniless and grief-stricken, Themistogenes leaves Syracuse and comes to the Greek colony of Metapontion, where he lives by his wits off the hospitality of a fat and lazy glutton called Hagnon. Hagnon takes a dilettante interest in philosophy, and Themistogenes supplies him with a suitably appreciative audience and a companion at table. At Hagnon's, Themistogenes meets a man from Issus known only as "The Issusite," the overseer of Hagnon's slaves and himself a slave. He is a man of learning and intelligence, who at the time of Themistogenes' arrival is deeply shaken by the death of his wife. The Issusite, later called Isias, decides to escape and attempts to murder Hagnon. Themistogenes intervenes to save Hagnon's life but does nothing to prevent the escape. Isias is shortly afterwards followed into hiding by a slave girl called Keria, who is admired by Themistogenes but has eyes only for Isias. Themistogenes is finally forced to leave Hagnon, after considerably overstaying his welcome, and he comes to Taras (present-day Taranto). Here he meets Isias and Keria and invites them to join him. The three of them then make their way to Athens. In Athens Themistogenes wonders how best to remedy his penniless state and decides to join his friend Xenophon, who has enlisted in the Hellene corps being recruited for Cyrus's army. Then follow the march to Cunaxa and the battle and death of Cyrus. The Greeks are in a difficult position and their position becomes precarious when their generals and captains are treacherously murdered. At this point Themistogenes persuades Xenophon to rally the despairing Greeks. Xenophon does so and, as one of their leaders, takes them to the Black Sea and Byzantium. In Byzantium Themistogenes parts company with Isias and Keria, who follow Xenophon further to Thrace. Themistogenes eventually ends up in Metapontion again where he takes over Hagnon's wife and estate, apparently poisoning Hagnon to achieve this. As an old man he sits on his estate writing his memoirs and trying to persuade Isias and Keria to visit him. Eventually they come, but they refuse to stay: they must keep on the run. At the end Thermistogenes is left isolated and alone.

The most obvious way in which the two stories of Klemens and Themistogenes are linked is by a similarity of theme: they describe the breaking-out from captivity, both physical and spiritual, and the conquest of grief and suffering. The various characters all exemplify some aspect of this.

First, Themistogenes. One desperate night in Asia, after the murder of the Greek generals, he sits in his tent and watches the smoke rising from the oil lamp. He reviews his life, seeing it "like a play" (352). He thinks of his imprisonment in Syracuse and then his success there and finally his overwhelming grief at the loss of his family. He escapes from the scene of this disaster and remembers "my almost blind journey to Metapontion" (353). His reason tells him that instead of moaning he should be thankful to have survived, and he tries to begin anew: "I collected myself about my physical core, my strong body and its impulses and desires" (354). He comes to a kind of working arrangement with his sorrow: "I would say now: I could see my grief. I watched it as you might a cloud driving across the sky or a whisp of smoke from a lamp ascending towards the ceiling. I saw the movements of grief. But in this sober watching I retained my grief, my sorrow, and it wasn't as it had been" (354). In a sense Themistogenes recovers from the disaster. His life starts on an upward curve which leads to the victory at Cunaxa. But then it is followed by the new grief at the discovery of Cyrus's death and the cataclysm of the officers' murders. Now he sees the smoke from the lamp curving downwards, "humbly, in subjection" (354). It seems to match his mood: "I asked myself if my years, now total-ing thirty-five, really were to curve downwards to nothingness here in Asia's meaninglessness" (354). He realizes too that he has not yet really come to terms with the events in Syracuse: "I had a strange thought; it came and disappeared and returned. I thought that I had not yet conquered my grief, that though I may have analyzed it I had not won a victory over it. And then I also thought of the others' grief, begun recently, forty-nine days before, and the fresh grief they and I now felt" (355). For the first time he under-stands what his captivity in Syracuse was really like and what his fellow prisoners must have felt, since he equates this captivity with the position of the Greeks in Asia, apparently hopelessly trapped in a strange continent, without any possibility of escape, faced by certain death. In these circumstances Themistogenes reveals for the first and only time in his life true greatness. He overcomes his own personal sorrow and disappointment and achieves a feeling of solidarity with the others which enables him to save them. The characteristic that prompts him to do this seems to be a sense of humor, or perhaps it is irony:

I got up and looked at Xenophon's face. When I looked at it I thought that he, like me still a young man, was already preparing himself for the end by his sleep: sleeping to be able to die rested, I thought with a smile.

And the smile which I felt cross my face was neither grief nor happiness. It was quite simply a smile that came from the depths of my nature and soul, or which one of the gods, whose existence I understand in a spiritual sense, placed on my face, stroked over my face like a caress. It came to me like a refreshing drink.   (356)

Themistogenes is encouraged to take stock of the situation, and he sees that the only possibility is armed resistance. He wakes up Xenophon and by appealing to his well-known superstition he persuades him not to give up. And Xenophon too is saved by a sense of irony:

[Xenophon] brushed his hand over his forehead, over his cheeks, his chin, his mouth. But the gods didn't place a smile there.

"Why are we sitting here without doing anything, Themistogenes? What are we waiting for? Death?"

"Suppose you were to make a speech, Xenophon," I suggested.

"Speech?"

And the smile came: "A speech?"   (358)

The Greeks are saved, and for Themistogenes this psychological victory over despair is to be compared to military victory. Writing his memoirs in Metapontion he notes: "It was forty-nine days after our winning the battle near Babylon. Soon we were to win a new victory which I consider to be very great, namely the victory over our grief" (333). The Greeks succeed in breaking out of encirclement; very much, Themistogenes observes, as men hacking their way to freedom out of a stone quarry.

Themistogenes is a man who triumphantly breaks out of captivity and despair. His friend Isias is another. When his wife dies Isias is overwhelmed with grief, but he uses his passion to make a bid for freedom. Themistogenes is present: "His face before all the lights in the room were extinguished showed deep grief. From it there arose an anger such as I have never seen in any other man's face: a man in grief, in despair and captivity liberating himself by anger" (372). However, physical liberation is only apparent liberation. When Themistogenes meets Isias and Keria in Taras they are in an abject state: "Their shadows were those of slaves" (183). Isias's real liberation occurs in Taras and is revealed when Themistogenes toys with the idea of selling him and Keria to raise money. Isias bursts out laughing when he hears of the scheme, and Themistogenes notes "the change that had occurred in him" (196). In the retreat through Asia Isias reveals that he is as capable of overcoming disappointment as Themistogenes is; there is a brief glimpse of him as a captain urging on his dispirited men through the Armenian snows. As a contrast to Isias and Themistogenes, who emerge from grief battered but fighting, there is Hagnon, a parody of self-pity. Hagnon too has lost his wife, as he never tires of telling everyone: "I have suffered a great deal. Few suspect it. I bear it without breaking. . . . And I have noticed that suffering ennobles us" (147). There is little that is noble about either Hagnon's physical appearance or his behavior. When he sits in the saddle he runs to the ground "like a kind of jellyfish" (108), while he consoles himself for the loss of his wife with young slave girls.

Krilon describes the *Anabasis* as "a tragedy whose proud arc. . . rises from hope towards even greater hope of victory, and then sinks towards defeat, flight, choruses of complaint. And we can also visualize the perfect climb of the next arc, yes, we can imagine how it rises towards the joy of coming home" (*Krilon Himself,* 519). In *The Clouds over Metapontion* the arc is shown descending again. For Themistogenes does not win any permanent peace when he comes back to Metapontion. He lives under the constant threat of an invasion from the north, a threat symbolized for him by the clouds that sweep in over the colony from the mountains in the north. Themistogenes himself changes. Not only does he occupy Hagnon's position—he also begins to resemble Hagnon. He sleeps with Hagnon's former slave mistresses and puts on weight, "though I am not such a slob as Hagnon was" he declares defensively (372). Isias is only too well aware that the old slaves become the new masters. Themistogenes reminds him of their glorious exploits in Asia:

> Then he mumbled something about our mutual differences, the quarrels of our soldiers and generals. "Those with power wanted to enslave the others, those who had given them that power," he said softly. I assume he did not mean me and the power I acquired.
> "But we fought our way out of captivity by our own efforts. And we were often victorious," I said.
> He replied: "Ultimately there cannot be any such thing as good victors."
> (403)

Victory has not brought happiness to Isias and Keria, and to Themistogenes it brings isolation and uneasiness: "It often seems to me that I am living alone on an island abandoned by others. Sometimes I call it Omega, the isle of finality, or the island of the watchful eye. I give it many names. Sometimes I call it the Isle of Endurance" (404).

The problems that Klemens faces are similar to those of Themistogenes. Man's physical conditions may change over the centuries but his spiritual existence does not. The thoughts and emotions of Ancient Greeks are completely relevant to the twentieth century. Professor Lévy indicates this when he says he investigates the past "to learn more about man's conditions on earth and his possibilities of fighting against suffering" (35). His widow sees the story as an encouragement: "It is mostly concerned with how difficult it was for men then, too, in war. But also (and there was triumph and resonance in her broken voice), but *also* with how we can survive!" (67). Klemens, on the other hand, is more inclined to view Themistogenes' final state as an awful warning: "It was a description of privation, of defeat, of victory, and finally anxiety. Did [Lévy] intend it as a warning? Of the horrible things man can discover, that ingenious and technical man can invent and that he wants to test, carry out experiments with?" (118).

Like Themistogenes Klemens is imprisoned and like him he manages to escape. Klemens too has to come to terms with the death of his wife and children and he too analyzes his grief without fully overcoming it. When he flies over the North Sea to England more than ten years after his wife's disappearance he is still tortured by the memory of his loss. In Metaponto he appears to achieve some stability: "These days were his best time since the spring of 1940. Not until now, he sometimes thought, had the war ended and the world—here—attained that incomprehensible state known as peace" (288). But he has merely suppressed his grief again. The clouds roll in from the north, the rain pours down, and he looks at the sea: "The sea was darker; memories rose from the sea. He felt hate for autumnal, wintry seascapes return and slink into his calm satisfaction. The years, the past that had concealed itself in forgetfulness and was something he had thrown away was eager to get at him again" (293). Klemens does not seem to be able to cope as well with his grief as Themistogenes. The same is true of Claire and Heinz. They may have escaped physically from a labor camp, but they have not won any real freedom. Heinz is scared that his past will catch up with him, while Claire's attachment to him is a symbol of her inability to escape a kind of slave mentality. Anxiety is as much the result of victory in the twentieth century as it was more than two thousand years earlier. When Klemens travels home past Metaponto "the plain looked like a lake. The low hills beneath him rose out of it like islands" (400), a description that foreshadows Themistogenes' talk of being isolated on an island. Klemens too shivers under threatening clouds, though now perhaps clouds of a more sinister nature, the results of "ingenious and technical man's" experiments, the hydrogen bomb.

The two stories in *The Clouds over Metapontion* are connected in so far as the problems the two sets of characters face are the same. Are there closer parallels? In a study of the narrative technique of the novel, Göransson claims: "It is difficult to get at the parallelism in the novel by investigating separate details; rather it is in their attitudes that the likenesses between the main characters in the novel are to be found."[5] This seems largely true, though there are parallels in detail between the three principal characters in each story. For example, both Klemens and Themistogenes have been prisoners of war and both have escaped. Both lose their wives and children through the activities of dictators; both try to come to terms with their grief; both finish up anxious and isolated. Both pursue, rather half-heartedly, a girl who in her turn pursues another man. Isias and Heinz have points of contact in that they are both former prison guards and their mistresses, Keria and Claire, are their former prisoners. There is some similarity in their names: Isias comes from Issus, Heinz from Alsace, Swedish *Elsass*; the same principle of consonance applies to Claire and Keria. But the basic pattern is disturbed by a—deliberate—imbalance. Can the admirable Isias really be compared to the unattractive Heinz? Can Keria, who is never really described, be compared to the lively Claire? And as far as the action is concerned, Klemens's journey to Sicily is not as remotely as exciting as the Persian expedition.

Though the two stories may not be exactly equated they are combined in other ways. Themistogenes' story is always present in Klemens's consciousness and so in his story. When in Taranto, Klemens remembers Themistogenes' stay there, and when he sees Claire the ages run into one another: "At first Klemens thought it was Cora, some Cora, but then Claire, and then another—what sort of dress had she?—a young woman who was 2381 years old. And then it was no one" (130). When he stands in the temple ruins at Metaponto a similar merging of times and persons occurs:

> It streamed into Klemens's memory now. That age, vanished long ago, became so close, like freedom, like the feeling of space and movement, and an unending and anyway so distant tragedy. And that feeling was mixed with, flowed like a tributary into the other: the recently, very recently vanished time, a time of imprisonment, despair, hate, and promises. When I get there, if I'm heading that way, I won't forget. He stood there (Who? Klemens? Lévy? Themistogenes of Syracuse and Athens? Someone—The Watcher?), he stood there in a loneliness that was not freedom from anything.
> (263)

The two stories run together in a more physical way in the novel, since they are shuffled both in order of internal event and with each other. This may serve the purpose of confusing the reader's sense of time, but it does not make the two stories into one. For example, in the final section of the book the account of the Greeks' retreat alternates with descriptions of Klemens's journey with Claire to Syracuse, though there does not seem to be any similarity between the two movements; rather, their conjunction emphasizes their difference. Sverker Göransson mentions another distinguishing feature: in the modern section of the novel everything is seen from Klemens's point of view, while there are several points of view adopted in the Greek story.[6] The result is that the variety of the Classical episodes is emphasized, while Klemens's story is even further restricted. In the end, Klemens becomes not so much a character in a parallel story as an observer of Themistogenes' life. This is possibly what Karl Vennberg may have had in mind in his review of *The Clouds over Metapontion:* "What ought to have contented itself with being a framework or the occasional reflection looms as a modern counterpart, a profound echo, and demands an attention it cannot hold."[7]

Perhaps the most interesting thing about Themistogenes is his relationship with Xenophon and the difference between his account of the Persian expedition and Xenophon's *Anabasis*. Themistogenes of Syracuse is mentioned in Xenophon's *Hellenica* (III, 1) as the author of an account of the Greeks' campaign with Cyrus. As Lévy explains, this is generally taken to be a joke; Themistogenes is merely a cover name for Xenophon himself. Lévy, however, thinks it would be fun to regard Themistogenes as a real man and writer, and he tries to reconstruct his life "as it could have been" (68). In the end the physical distinction between Themistogenes and Xenophon is blurred. When Isias first sees them together he thinks they look like "a couple of brothers, though differently dressed" (204). Later, when they are dressed alike, they are "difficult to distinguish at a distance" (235). And when Themistogenes persuades Xenophon to deliver his crucial speech, he claims almost to have created him: "I seemed to see Xenophon born of my spirit, of my dream" (359).

Themistogenes is careful to distinguish his account of events from Xenophon's: "We saw more or less the same things. But the observations and memories I carry with me cannot be the same as his. They have been purified or contaminated by me and not by him" (194). Yet the account reproduced in *The Clouds over Metapontion* differs very little from that of the *Anabasis*. Johnson's story is concerned principally with the march inland, the battle of Cunaxa, and the emergence of Xenophon as a leader; that is, the first three books of the seven books of the *Anabasis*. It is rather surprising that the dramatic journey through Armenia to the sea (Book VI) is dismissed in a couple of pages, only the march through the snow and the celebrated glimpse of the Black Sea receiving more than a cursory mention. The remaining books of the *Anabasis* are only referred to indirectly, and then in connection with Isias. Johnson alters almost nothing of Xenophon's story, though there are of course differences caused by the insertion of three extra characters: Themistogenes, Isias, and Keria. Occasionally Johnson adds information not in Xenophon's story, either solid fact, such as the course of the Wall of Media (322; *Anabasis* II, 4), or artistic decoration, such as the physical attractions of Queen Epyaxa (208; *Anabasis* I, 2).

Johnson tends to take a more jaundiced view of soldiers' behavior than Xenophon. When the troops come to a river full of large, tame fish worshiped as gods by the Syrians (*Anabasis* I, 4), Johnson adds brutally: "The soldiers grilled them and thought they tasted good" (219). He is also less enthusiastic about Cyrus than Xenophon is. When Cyrus destroys a beautiful orchard, Xenophon does not comment (*Anabasis* I, 4), while Themistogenes expresses displeasure (219). But these are only minor differences. In fact, Johnson follows Xenophon so closely that where Xenophon has an obituary chapter on Cyrus (*Anabasis* I, 9), Themistogenes writes: "In Proxenos's re-erected tent Xenophon began rather unexpectedly to talk about Cyrus's life" (250). A similar technique is applied to Xenophon's obituaries of the murdered generals (351; *Anabasis* II, 6).

The *Anabasis* is Johnson's main source for the historical part of his novel, but it is not the only one. Johnson seems to have read widely round the subject of the Greek colonies in Italy and the March of the Ten Thousand, and he has described his sometimes lengthy search for suitable literature on the subject.[8] A list of authorities and authors is ingeniously inserted in the novel, as a vision seen in Taranto by the none-too-sober Klemens (154). Paradoxically, the characters and society recreated out of this historical research are much more vital and interesting than the author's compatriot and contemporary Klemens, in surroundings that Johnson has himself experienced.[9] This judgment is confirmed by all the other novels Johnson has written since the war.

CHAPTER 7

Tyrants and Lovers

I Dreams of Roses and Fire

JOHNSON'S greatest achievement since the war is represented by three novels in historical settings: *Drömmar om rosor och eld* (*Dreams of Roses and Fire*, 1949), *Hans nådes tid* (*The Days of His Grace*, 1960), and *Livsdagen lång* (*Life's Long Day*, 1964). They are the stories of men and women who devote themselves to love against a background of war and oppression. Their plans are thwarted and their desires frustrated in a power game where they can only be pawns and victims. Love, however, survives somehow to give their lives meaning and to help them preserve their human dignity in the face of overwhelming odds.

Dreams of Roses and Fire is set in seventeenth-century France, "in the town of L. in what is now the *departement* of Vienne" (7). In 1617 a new Catholic priest comes to the town—the handsome, eloquent, and overweening Urbain Grainier. He quickly makes enemies of some of the leading male citizens, who resent his arrogance and envy his success with women. Later he also annoys the women by being obstinately faithful to his mistress, Madeleine de Brone, and no longer seducing them. His enemies combine to get rid of him but they fail and are humiliated. A further source of conflict is the destruction of the city walls. Cardinal Richelieu, the virtual ruler of France, has determined to destroy all former Huguenot fortifications, and the town of L. is one of his victims. A group of citizens, including Grainier, fight to preserve the town, while Richelieu's supporters bitterly oppose them. A band of Ursuline nuns settle in the town and under their new prioress, Sister Jeanne, they begin to feel strange desires. Their confessor, Jehan Minet, suspects they are possessed by devils and calls in a professional exorcist, Pierre Barrot. Barrot forces the devils to reveal that they have been set on the nuns by Grainier. Seizing this opportunity, all Grainier's enemies, from Richelieu downwards, combine to have the priest condemned for sorcery. They are led by Richelieu's representative, Laubardemont. Grainier refuses to accept a chance to escape and despite torture he will not confess to the crime of witchcraft. His enraged and baffled accusers finally drag him to the stake and burn him as a heretic in the city square.

The frame round this story is political and personal persecution— or in more modern terms, "a case of liquidation" (317). At the heart of the story is the priest Urbain Grainier, a man who chooses martyr-dom as a weapon to defeat his opponents.

Grainier recognizes three faults in his character: pride, desire for power, and lust for women. All three are responsible for bringing about his death. His disastrous pride naturally makes him enemies, and he is then too proud to compromise or be reconciled with them. In a church procession, for example, he claims the right to precede the Bishop of Luçon; unfortunately, the enraged bishop is the future Cardinal Richelieu. When Grainier defeats his enemies in their first campaign against him he rubs in their humiliation by reentering the town in a triumphal procession with a laurel branch in his hand. As far as ordinary people are concerned, he can feel no sympathy or understanding for them, only contempt: "How could I love a flock of sheep other than as an entertainment?" (148). He only wants power over them, power to provoke either admiration or hatred, but some response at any rate. He enjoys the sense of power that women's infatuation with him provides. When the demented nuns scream their desires at him he observes: "What moved me and fright-ened me, and, I must admit, attracted me and in a way flattered me, were the sounds from the women's throats. I felt a kind of power when I heard them" (364). It is a dangerous power, and Grainier is not the man to wield it with compassion. As Madeleine puts it: "God has given you a face and body that may not suit your soul" (28). Representative of Grainier's victims is Philippe Tranchant, daughter of one of his best friends. He seduces her and then abandons her to a broken father, an illegitimate child, and a loveless, face-saving marriage.

For Grainier life is basically a game. He does not live so much as act. He has chosen to play the part of defender of the city walls. When Madeleine begs him to forgive and forget he replies:

"I am defending myself. And I have to win. If I don't win—time and time again—then I am lost. There is no middle way, no compromise for me. Not any more."

"Urbain, you could leave all this," she said.

"I could be a soldier and kill with weapons. I could have joined in a war and become a general and killed Huguenots or others. I could have followed the Cardinal's troops to La Rochelle and joined in the Cardinal's game, or followed Duke Rohan and played in his team. But I stayed here and played my own game to save the city walls and fortifications and myself, and it is a game that is already lost. I am not lost as long as I play my game—even if the game is lost. I am myself, I remain alive."   (26–27)

In this game it is attitudes and poses that are important. When Grainier meets one of his persecutors, Minet, he strikes a pose for him so that "every picture other than that belonging to this moment should go to the future as wrong and a caricature" (270). It is appearances that count, not the reality—if there is such a thing— behind them.

Grainier's conception of life as the consistent playing of a chosen role and his awareness that the spectators will not worry over- much about the actor behind the mask, determine his reaction to events. As he faces death he writes in his journal:

There exist now: Laubardemont, Madeleine, and God.

Laubardemont is my instrument, my means of attaining my dignity, that of the fighting martyr. Without him I might only be a refugee.

Madeleine is my wife and the meaning in my life and my death. All the tenderness I may have is directed at her.

God is my firm principle, He is a means for me, a support . . . . God exists and is with me. He is an act of will. He contributes to my dignity, He is its foundation.

I am now the most powerful man in the town I once called mine, and that gives me a happiness I cannot deny.   (373–74)

It is because of his love for Madeleine and his faith in God that Grainier cannot escape his persecutors and so is forced to take on the role of "the fighting martyr." When he lies in bed with Madeleine and confesses his sins and innermost thoughts he declares: "I can- not leave you and I cannot leave God. I can forge you together at certain moments, now, to something giving me security and love. I am equipped for that. I am equipped up to that point. But if I leave God I am lost, discarded, without a foothold. I cannot leave you, for then I am destroyed" (329). Madeleine is love, but scarcely security; God is security, but not love. The very nature of Grainier's love for Madeleine is insecurity, a love born in spiritual terror and ending in physical obliteration. He has secretly married Made- leine and justified his action by writing a pamphlet criticizing the

Church's ruling on celibacy. At the end of his life he believes his relationship with Madeleine is right, but at the time he married her in fear and trembling: "When I claimed that we were guiltless *then*—I lied. I didn't believe we were guiltless. I believed we were lost" (330). Their love is an emotion that must be nurtured by danger and fear. When Madeleine suggests they flee the town, he knows it is impossible. Risk is the essence of their love for one another, and if they escape from danger then they will lose their mutual respect and be abandoned to ever increasing boredom: "We should be a middle-aged couple on the run and nothing else" (321). Madeleine provides the emotional tension in Grainier's life; God is "the firm principle." And Grainier's conception of God is highly abstract and devoid of emotion. God is "an act of will," a concept that Grainier appears almost to create because he cannot live without such a concept. He compares himself to Galileo, who is at that moment being charged with heresy. Galileo has the possibility of explaining the world in scientific, mathematical terms; but Grainier, ignorant of mathematics, would be exposed to nihilism if he were to abandon his belief in God: "I have no theoretical possibility of doubting" (329). The priesthood is a role for him, just as the defense of the walls is. He must play it consistently to the end. That is another reason for his not being able to escape, for to do so he would have to adopt a less satisfactory role: " 'There are only prisons,' he said. 'To escape—for me—is to change cells. Living the life of a renegade priest is also a prison. Living the life of a soldier is a prison. There is most peace in the Church's. . . . I find the balance I need in the Church' " (28–29).

Grainier cannot escape, but he is not the man to lie down and accept his fate. Instead his arrogance and love of power lead him to a remarkable conclusion: that by going to the stake he can win a crushing and irreversible victory over his enemies. By presenting himself as "the fighting martyr" he will win the future, generation after generation, to his side, and his persecutors will be condemned as sadists and villains to the end of history. Laubardemont, the unquestioning servant and tool of a dictator, is the man who makes his role possible, for nothing can justify Laubardemont's role. Grainier rehearses his part carefully so that he can make the right impression at the trial and the execution. He steels himself for the final torture during the preliminary investigations, and he does not "confess" when it comes. He discovers that by pretending to forgive his enemies he can reduce them to impotent rage. When his jailer's wife comes in and swears at him, he declares sweetly that he forgives her. She bursts into tears: "I felt joy, triumph. I felt what great power I still have. I felt more strongly than ever that I had found the principle and means" (372). Grainier plays his role perfectly to the end, and his resistance provokes his interrogators to greater and greater bestiality and a worse and worse reputation in the eyes of the future.

Grainier's understanding of his emotions and his motives is astonishingly clear, and it is this that distinguishes him from his opponents. They do not or will not understand their reasons for wanting Grainier burnt. The two ostensible reasons for removing Grainier are his opposition to the demolishing of the city walls and his witchcraft, but these are essentially reasons people persuade themselves they believe. Grainier observes: "I became an obstacle to those who wanted to demolish. But if they had looked into themselves they would have discovered that I wasn't an obstacle—or only a minor obstacle. They have not looked into themselves" (353). It is the same with the devils. When Grainier meets Minet he asks him if he *really* believes in the devils in the Ursuline sisters: "Go down into the depths of your being, Minet, and question and probe. No, you won't do it. You want to believe in the demons" (271). Those who want to believe Grainier is guilty succeed in persuading themselves that he is, even when they themselves fabricate the evidence for his guilt. Their minds work on two different levels. Richelieu is a good example of this phenomenon. He has good personal reasons for getting rid of Grainier: he wants the walls to be razed to humiliate the Huguenots and to provide building material for his new town of Richelieu nearby; he has an old grudge to settle as the Bishop of Luçon. Yet it is not at all impossible that he believes in Grainier's guilt. The author says of Richelieu: "When he was asked on his deathbed, so it is said, if he forgave his enemies, he is supposed to have replied that he did not have any enemies and had never felt enmity for others than the enemies of the State. All through his life he kept his childhood faith, that is, he believed in demons. Adjacent to this faith, as a subdivision of it, was his insight into how superstition and even genuine faith can be used and exploited in the general service" (318). The same attitude is displayed by the two priests, Minet and Barrot, who patently engineer the rousing and abjuring of the devils. They have obvious personal reasons for hating Grainier. They are both deformed and so resent Grainier's sexual successes; but they are adept at denying unpleasant facts, concealing them from themselves. They cannot connect their convenient discovery of the devils with their desire to be rid of Grainier. The poor nuns are even less aware that their denunciations of Grainier are the result of hate, born of frustrated desire; with the exception of Sister Jeanne they are completely carried away by their emotions. Passion is, in fact, the quality that distinguishes *Dreams of Roses and Fire*; no other book of Johnson's seems to burn with such an intensity. Johnson's heroes are usually reflective and ironical, not a bit like Grainier. Grainier compares his situation with that of Galileo, whose ironic recantation of heresy is printed at the beginning of the novel, and in *The Days of His Grace* it is the Galileo type that predominates. Here, however, Grainier goes out in a blaze of emotion, the master and victim of passions that are symbolized by roses and their scent: "Men die out, most of them through fire. Doubtless many die through flowers, but that is also through fire. The fire of their slow or violent fragrance, of love, and of hate" (21).

Although the story is set in seventeenth-century France, it is not in fact so strictly confined in time and space. Basic to the whole is the interplay of past and future: the twentieth-century author and his readers gaze at these seventeenth-century characters, and they peer anxiously back. This strange communication across three centuries is expressed in several ways. Firstly, there are the mechanics of storytelling. The story is told by a modern author— he calls it "my story" (319)—and also through the eyes of a contemporary diarist, Daniel Drouin. Drouin is a gourmet, a man with a certain pride in his knowledge of Latin, and a liberal who in the final analysis is too frightened to stand up and support his old friend Grainier. Drouin's account is influenced by his desire to present his behavior in the best possible light, and it is necessary to read between the lines. The author himself does not claim to give a completely accurate account of what happened, since it is so difficult to interpret the relevant documents: "Much age has gathered in their folds" (189). A particular obstacle to understanding the past is the difference in psychological insight between now and then. Sister Jeanne looks across three centuries and says: "You can say: 'We know much more now about such things.' I can reply that

I experienced all this but it can't be fully told" (105). She has to explain her frustrations and temptations in terms of devils. The author may have a more precise terminology at his disposal, but his understanding is not necessarily greater: "How should we at this early stage of man's history, we who haven't advanced beyond the atomic bomb, be capable of surveying cause and effect in such a delicate network and such sensitive material as nerves and souls?" (102). However, the dialogue between past and future goes deeper than the question of interpretation. Grainier plans his victory not in his own time but in the future. He explains this to Minet, who comes to tell him to escape before it is too late. Grainier argues that Minet is trying to save himself by such a maneuver. Every judge is in an unenviable position, as much a prisoner as the man he judges, for his judgment will in its turn be judged. Grainier points out it has taken the Church twenty years to come to a decision about Galileo, so scared are his judges of making fools of themselves in the eyes of the future: "We are afraid of posterity, whatever we may say about it and however much we pretend to express our indifference, even our contempt, for what it may think" (273). Considering his own case, Grainier sees that Richelieu will have an excuse when the future comes to judge him, for he can claim to be building up a state: "We appeal to the future's judgment with our results and not with our morals" (275). But Laubardemont will be condemned, for he is merely a willing tool, and the same condemnation will be applied to Minet, for his results will not be sufficiently impressive to justify his actions. What then is the future's, the author's, judgment? Of Richelieu: "He left a great inheritance. We can consider it was good or bad, that it was a mixture of both, that it was filled with casual or planned and coldly executed cruelty, with a breadth or narrowness of vision, blood, death, building up and pulling down. But we cannot deny it was great" (318). But of Laubardemont: "He was a relatively powerful but not significant figure. . . . In addition, we know he did not survive, that he was incapable of being saved. He is covered in a shame that no one can ever wash off, his skeleton rests in shame, his memory cannot be honored by anyone" (320). All the main characters are aware that they will be judged at the tribunal of time. Even poor, neutral Daniel Drouin polishes and revises the entries in his diary, for it is "a report intended for the future that will judge all of us" (124).

Johnson's story is not an invention. It is based on events in the town of Loudun, involving a priest called Urbain Grandier.[1] Not a great deal seems to be changed, though in the interests of limiting the cast Johnson allows Minet and Barrot to play the roles of interrogator throughout, whereas in fact two other priests were responsible for Grandier's final torturing. Johnson disclaims responsibility for writing a completely historical account by changing the names of the characters, though only slightly. For example, Minet was actually called Mignon and Barrot was called Barré. Some of the more unlikely episodes are actually taken from historical documents—for example, the appearance of a cat at one of the exorcism ceremonies. Daniel Drouin is preserved for posterity only by his outburst at this ceremony against the ungrammatical Latin used by the devils; Johnson's development of his character is purely fictitious. The same historical incidents have been described by an English author, Aldous Huxley, in *The Devils of Loudun* (1952). Huxley's interpretation of Richelieu's role corresponds closely with Johnson's: "Laubardemont and his tame magistrates were the agents of a man who was not concerned with fact, or logic, or law, or theology, but only with personal vengeance and a political experiment, carefully designed to show how far, in this third decade of the seventeenth century, the methods of totalitarian dictatorship could safely be pushed" (230–31).[2] It is this aspect of the episode that makes it more than a historical curiosity. *Dreams of Roses and Fire* is very much "a novel about the present."

II *"Living on an Aspen Leaf—"*

The action of *The Days of His Grace* takes place in the Europe of Charlemagne, the king of the Franks who became the first of the Holy Roman Emperors and who towers above the Dark Ages as a soldier, politician, and patron of learning. Charlemagne's achievements, like Richelieu's, are impressive, but as with Richelieu, Johnson prefers to describe the emperor from the point of view of one of his victims: the Lupigis family, from Forojuli in the Kingdom of Lombardy (present-day Cividale in the Italian province of Friuli).

The story begins with a storm on the Adriatic at the end of Lent, A.D. 775. Anselm Lupigis, a deacon, rides out the storm in a boat, while his brother Bertoald and his three nephews, Warnefrit, Conald, and Johannes, experience it in Forojuli. It is the year after

Charlemagne's destruction of the power of the Kingdom of Lombardy and the Lombards are still smarting under the blow. They spend their evenings talking about their former glory and reviling the Franks. When the storm reaches Forojuli the Lupigis family are gathered for such an evening in the castle of Duke Rodgaud. Young Johannes, sixteen years old and still affectionately called Johanniperto, is sitting in front of the fire with Rodgaud's slightly younger daughter Angila when a sudden gust of wind blows a spark into Angila's lap. Johannes quickly extinguishes it with his hand, but it has ignited passions that determine the lives of the main characters. When Johannes touches Angila's thigh they both realize for the first time the nature of sexuality, and desire is sparked off between them. Their mutual discovery is witnessed by Warnefrit and Conald, who are consumed by jealousy, and by Rodgaud, who is furious. A temporary diversion is caused by the arrival of Anselm, who delivers some thoroughly ambiguous remarks on the political situation and entertains the villagers with tales from Lombard history. After Anselm's departure the Lupigis brothers' rivalry over Angila becomes so intense that it results in Conald's precipitous departure, while Rodgaud's anger finds outlet in preparations for a revolt against Charlemagne.

The revolt is launched a year later and is crushed almost before it has begun. The result is catastrophe: Bertoald and Warnefrit are carried off into captivity, and while Johannes himself survives, he loses Angila, who is carted off as a bride by Gunderic, the brutish notary acting as Charlemagne's representative in the mopping-up operations. The ensuing story is one of desolation, misery, and bitterness, with brief moments of happiness, as the characters are tossed about in the storms of Charlemagne's empire building. Soldiers and politicians rock the world; lesser mortals try desperately to maintain some sort of foothold. As the motto at the beginning of the novel expresses it: "Living on an aspen leaf—. No one can live in security on an aspen leaf. Yet there are small insects who do not know their world is an aspen leaf. For them it is a home, a homeland in the world, the world of the aspen leaf" (7). The characters all develop in similar ways: resistance, followed by imprisonment, resulting in submission or resignation. Bertoald Lupigis takes part in Rodgaud's revolt, is imprisoned, and released when he shows that he is no longer dangerous. He never returns to Forojuli, being swept away by an avalanche on the journey home;

but Warnefrit returns on his release to the farm in Forojuli and behaves as a loyal servant of the emperor. Conald fights against Charlemagne in Bavaria, is captured, and becomes a soldier in the Frankish army. Racked by toothache, he drags out a wretched existence of drunkenness and brawls, until on the northern marches of the empire a Danish arrow puts him out of his misery. Johannes plots to kill Charlemagne, is imprisoned, and then enters the king's service to become royal secretary. Angila becomes hard and bitter in her forced marriage; eventually she tries to escape, but Gunderic fetches her back and holds her prisoner. Johannes comes to release her, and together at last they ride back to Forojuli. But Angila, now mild and reconciled to life, is too weak and dies on the way. Love is the only thing that survives the upheavals in the characters' lives. The love that springs up between Johannes and Angila in Rodgaud's castle follows them to their deaths, thwarted perhaps, but not destroyed by the processes of despotism.

In Johnson's novels surface events are usually only a dramatic representation of the underlying ideas. To understand the principles behind *The Days of His Grace* it is necessary first to examine what Anselm tells the sullen Lombards in Forojuli and second to pursue the career of Johannes Lupigis.

Anselm is devious in his pronouncements, and what he really means is a matter for conjecture. He attempts to dissuade the Lombards from reacting to the Franks' occupation of Lombardy by armed revolt. The Lombards, he says, should work together with Charlemagne. On the other hand, he criticizes those who are too eager to give up their independence and become submerged in the empire the Franks are creating. Perhaps Anselm foresees the future structure of Europe, the alliance between Church and State, Pope and Emperor, symbolized by Charlemagne's coronation in the Church of St. Peter, Rome, A.D. 800. Johannes wonders: "Did he want to entice them closer to Rome, or closer to the king of the Franks? Closer to both, to a stronger union with both?" (63). The question marks are typical of the doubt that surrounds Anselm's motives. However, if the Lombards are to be merely a vassal state in a great empire, how can they preserve any kind of independence? Clearly they cannot maintain any political independence, but Anselm seems to suggest that there is some sort of spiritual independence open to them, if they can preserve a consciousness of their past, their Lombard heritage. Anselm himself is anxious to

record Lombard history, and in Forojuli he sets about collecting
stories and reminiscences with the ultimate aim of writing a history
of his people. He is equally concerned that the others should be
aware of their inheritance and in the evenings he regales his listeners
with tales from their past:

> It was as if he took hold of the endlessly flowing fabric of time, held it
> awhile between his hands and like a weaver presented it for inspection,
> bit by bit. He let his listeners calmly study the past.
> "Our people's past piles itself up in front of us," he said. "*In front of us.*
> It's beginning to become too much for us. It's like great mounds of leaves
> in the fall, like enormous drifts of leaves. Soon we'll be trampling in it as
> in a compost heap. We have to wade through it again, although it ought
> to lie behind us. We've certainly lived through it and made our marks on
> it and gotten marks from it—our people has lived through everything.
> Now the time has come for us to consume again what we've experienced,
> swallow it whatever it may taste like, so as to be free of things in the past
> that might still hurt us. You think it sounds odd. But that's the law of
> life and the law of knowledge, that's how we acquire clarified experience."
>   (72)

"Clarified experience" is the clue to Anselm's arguments. The
Lombards must be aware of their past, but their knowledge must
be clarified—not sullied by impetuous emotional reactions. They
must not be misled by their awareness of the past into comparing
their former power with their present subjection, as they have been
doing. That is an example of how the past can still hurt them, when
it is not properly digested. If they examine their own history they
will find that they were once in a similar position to the Franks,
when they established the Kingdom of Lombardy, and they behaved
with equal cruelty towards their subject peoples.

Not all Lombards are able to develop a proper sense of historical
perspective. Rodgaud is one who does not, and though his rebellion
is easily put down, others fail to heed the warning and even twenty-
five years later the emperor's son is forced to quell a Lombard
uprising: "Dukes and dukes' sons who lacked the necessary talent
for forgetting in the right way still dreamed of great power for the
Lombard people" (531). It is this "talent for forgetting" that Anselm
is trying to encourage, but he seems to mean rather more than just
letting bygones be bygones: "Everywhere, continually, he produced
the word 'peace.' But long afterwards it was said he also had other
words on his tongue, whispered words such as 'treachery,' 'murder,'

'our people,' 'our own country,' 'our slow, calculated, outwardly invisible revenge' " (108). The apparent contradiction in Anselm's statements is explained in the story of his nephew, Johannes Lupigis.

Johannes takes part in Rodgaud's rebellion, but he knows full well it is doomed to failure. When the Franks arrive he escapes up into the mountains above Utina and there he understands what Anselm had been trying to say:

> He saw. We are defeated. He saw. When he thought of his people's history he was certain that they were defeated for good . . . . Perhaps new uprisings would be forced out of their enslavement, out of their hearts. They would be struck down again. The uprisings would be like the blind wandering of sleepwalkers towards ruin and a fearful awakening. Surviving, he thought. What has the possibility of surviving is the spirit we possess, that some of us possess. It can develop knowledge about life and learning from manuscripts. What is otherwise left for us is to cultivate the soil we are allowed to keep or to serve in foreign armies. To exist. To belong to a Frankish kingdom that grows larger and larger. (234–35)

The three possibilities open to the defeated Lombards are exemplified by the Lupigis brothers: Warnefrit is the farmer; Conald, the soldier; and Johannes, the scholar. Johannes sees why Anselm is interested in preserving written records of Lombard history and he devotes himself to the same task. For they can undermine the Franks from within. By producing a *History of the Lombards,* by lecturing on Lombardy at the Carolingian court schools, they can transmit Lombard culture and thought until it thoroughly pervades the culture of the Franks. Scholarship is to them what the picture of the coronation of the Emperor of China is to Krilon— a fifth column, the weapon of their "outwardly invisible revenge." Anselm and Johannes are well aware of a precedent for their action: the survival of Roman culture among the barbarian tribes that physically destroyed the Roman Empire. Both Anselm and Johannes use the Latin language, both are deeply influenced by Latin literature, and both have been educated by a Roman tutor, the aged Flavianus.

Although Johannes accepts the fate of his nation as he sits up among the mountains gazing at the moon, he is unable to come to terms with his own situation, for he is completely overwhelmed by the realization that he has lost Angila. Up on the moonlit mountainside he feels "proximity" (233), proximity to the Heavens above him

and proximity to Hell in the smoking, war-ravaged valley beneath
him. In his despair he longs to escape from the earth, and he feels
himself borne towards the moon. For a while he finds peace on
the moon, but glances from earth—particularly from Angila—
distract him, and the moon then begins to show displeasure. He is
thrown off into space and lands back on earth beneath a bush, on
a ledge that has arrested his fall from the mountain: "Beneath me
is the Underworld. The blessing of space is distant. The powers
of the Underworld reach me. My position—. My position is between
the two worlds" (245).

Johannes has discovered that the escapism represented by his
moon journey is impossible for him: he is too earthbound. But
before he can assume his natural position on earth, between Heaven
and Hell, he must continue his fall, descend into Hell as he ascended
into Heaven. His descent into the Underworld comes about because
he is unable to apply to his own personal past the sober reflection
he has devoted to his people's history. He is so blinded by his memories of Angila that he makes a solemn promise to kill Charlemagne.

Charlemagne has a most efficient network of spies; Johannes
comes under suspicion and is thrown into prison: "I lived near to
what I would call the Underworld, within the region which is rightly
designated as the kingdom of The Tempter" (461). Johannes is
faced with a dilemma: should he keep to his promise to kill Charlemagne and spend the rest of his life in a dungeon, or should he make
the best of a bad job, become Charlemagne's servant, and live a
materially comfortable life? At first he sticks to his principles, and
he is helped by the memory of a scent that comes to him in his cell
and which he finally identifies as the fragrance of the bush from the
mountain where he made his promise. The bush becomes a link with
his idealism. In the darkness of his cell he lets his imagination create
the bush again and again, a ritual that totally absorbs his thoughts
and energies. Finally, however, his creative strength fails and the
bush disappears. In a last desperate effort to assert his resistance he
denies God, denies Charlemagne, declares his support for the Saxon
rebels—but he cannot in the end avoid his descent into the kingdom
of The Tempter.

The Devil points out to Johannes the futility of his pledge to
kill Charlemagne. It condemns him to mouldering away forgotten
in captivity. The Devil says he can give him freedom, "all the freedom
a man needs in our enlightened times" (499) as he puts it, and make

him the king's secretary. Johannes resists: "*'No!'* said Johanniperto Lupigis from Forojuli and the mountains above Utina" (499). But the more mature Johannes soon realizes he is lost, tempted by food, by women, by life. When he is released from prison he expresses his fall from grace with this melancholy reflection: "You are like a branch, bending like the burnt crosier of a bishop down into the fire. The fresh branch that was you when you were cast into the fire bends downwards thus. Whose fire? You are alive, but the crosier has become ashes" (506). Johannes has been forced to sacrifice his ideals to the necessity of staying alive.

In time Johannes advances to the post of royal secretary and adopts the obliging smile of a courtier, a smile "well practiced, created in inner resistance" (273). He cannot influence events; his role is that of the passive spectator, the listener. But even if he is forced to conceal his opposition to Charlemagne, he does not forget it. The greatest threat to freedom is forgetfulness. Up in the mountains after Rodgaud's revolt he has thought of what his tutor Flavianus has told him:

Doors that previously stood open are slowly, ever so slowly closed; the hinges do not creak, there is no sound of scraping. Scarcely anyone hears or sees it, so slowly are they closed. But suddenly, or gradually, no one can say when or how, those shut in and those shut out know that the doors are closed and have been like that for some time—a year?—two years?—ten years?—have been like that since a long while back. Those growing up say that they've always been like that. After all, the fact that the doors are closed *is* freedom. They shut out a kind of unfreedom . . . . Hate itself dies. It is fixed in time and directly bound to memory. What are we to hate, what was it, what was it called? What did it look like? Are we unfree? Don't know. What's freedom, father, mother, teacher? Something to do with doors? Oh, is that all, wasn't it more? (236–37)

History can keep the ideal of freedom alive; memory can nourish hate. Not the hate that leads to futile resistance and life imprisonment, but "a nobler hate" (104), a spiritual hate preserved beneath a courtier's smile. Memory, like history, must be purified and clarified before it can play its role. Johannes describes the process when he looks back to the period of his imprisonment: "I have tried and succeeded in this—to penetrate into memories of pain to dissolve them in contemplation. To penetrate into the past so that I am there; and I am there now, and I say: The memory is *there* and it belongs to the living, it belongs to life in the present" (441).

Many of Johnson's characters try to come to terms with their bitter memories, from *Remembering* onwards, but few succeed like Johannes. Poor Angila sits in Gunderic's castle trying desperately to suppress her memories of Johannes, but Johannes can remember Angila calmly and yet with passion. The memory of Angila is a constant reminder to him of the nature of the man and powers he serves. This is brought out particularly at the coronation in St. Peter's, a scene whose importance is emphasized by its introducing the whole novel. Seeing the sparks of light thrown out by the precious stones in the imperial crown Johannes is reminded of other sparks and the storm that caused them:

I thought, if only for a moment, of this storm when at the end of last year I witnessed from an advantageous position the sudden and dignified crowning of our excellent King Carolus as emperor in the Church of St. Peter in Rome. I whispered to myself then: "Johannes, remember!" And the strange thing is that my fleeting thought made use of my childhood name, my petname there at home in Forojuli, and employed our Lombard language: "Johanniperto, Perto, you are in *fornaccar,* in the field that has been harvested, but never forget! The *faida* of the air and sea, this feud between powers of which we know no more than their strength and ruthlessness, this arbitrary power of the air, this wildly plowing *plovus,* remember it!"

I heard my own voice from then and my voice from now whisper: "Perto, surely you haven't forgotten?"

I replied in a whispering towards what is long since vanished or is at any rate hidden now: "No. It all remains. It is dormant. My hand is in the service of the emperor, and in my mind there is peace."   (15)

"It is dormant." Johannes never loses sight of his ideals, even if he is forced to compromise. He remains an optimistic figure in the sense that the ideas and thoughts he grafts onto the Frankish Empire must eventually bear fruit, but in the short term he can only quietly record the inhumanity of his master and his political system—despotism. Johannes is a scholarly, determined, but somewhat disillusioned character as he stands looking in the mirror with his head slightly inclined to one side: "A listener's head, where with the passing of years the smile dies, fades like a consumed fire—as the mirror is lowered while the roar increases, while fiercer and fiercer winds blow through the forest, the roar of the prisoners' shrieks in the kingdom of His Grace, My Lord, Our Emperor Carolus Magnus" (273).

The author of *The Days of His Grace* purports to draw on the commentary of a monk called Agibert, whom he calls "our compiler" (525). Agibert is a friend and contemporary of Johannes and on Johannes's death he sets out to write his life story. Agibert regards himself as a scholar and historian whose aim is to get at the truth, and *The Days of His Grace,* like several of Johnson's works, is also the story of the writing of the story as Agibert sifts and interprets the evidence. He draws on Johannes's own memoirs, he studies the annals of the imperial secretary Einhard, and he conducts an on-the-spot investigation in Forojuli. The author then takes over where Agibert has to leave off. The author can reproduce conversations, report streams of consciousness, that the historian cannot claim to know of. The division of labor between author and historian is to some extent reflected in the style of the novel. Passages which are supposed to be extracts from the eighth or ninth centuries are written in a language that is old-fashioned and mannered, both in vocabulary and syntax. Other sections, particularly passages of dialogue or internal monologues, are in more modern, colloquial Swedish. [3]

The most important stylistic features of the novel are irony and feigned ignorance. Agibert and Johannes are writing in a totalitarian state and must exercise extreme care. When Johannes looks back to Rodgaud's rebellion, he writes: "My hand is hesitant and in the service of the emperor" (191). When Agibert comes to the question of Johannes's guilt in plotting against Charlemagne, he pauses: "I, Agibertus, dare not describe anything or even make clearer guesses in this difficult subject" (418). Consequently, *The Days of His Grace* is a novel of some subtlety that demands careful reading, preferably, perhaps, by a trained kremlinologist. There are ways round censorship. There is the irony of flattery or understatement, such as when Johannes describes the Franks' treatment of Forojuli: "Truly our present emperor showed mildness. We were allowed to retain a remarkably large number of horses, considerable quantity of cattle and sufficient servants and slaves. In our district only a small number of farms were burned" (217). Another device is for the writer to say what he thinks and then immediately disclaim responsibility for it. This develops at times into a game in which the author refuses to make definite statements and instead expresses himself in questions and guesses, as in his treatment of Anselm in Forojuli.

Johnson has clearly devoted some time to research into the reality behind *The Days of His Grace*. Like Agibert he combined field studies with the reading of historical documents. He has described some of his on-the-spot researches in *Vägar över Metaponto* (*Roads via Metaponto*, 1959);[4] the epitaph Johannes places over Angila's grave is taken from a gravestone in the museum in Zurich. His reading had to be pursued, through lack of Latin, in German translations.[5] The tales that Anselm tells from Lombard history are nearly all taken from Paul the Deacon's celebrated *History of the Lombards*, a book Johnson apparently first discovered in Berlin in 1923.[6] In a postscript to *The Days of His Grace* Johnson notes that Anselm may "fleetingly" (587) remind readers of Paul—in fact, the resemblance seems to be considerably more than fleeting. Paul's history is largely based on the work of Gregory of Tours, and Anselm too draws on Gregory's book, praising the bishop as "a fresh and clear spring for all who seek knowledge" (96). For the later part of the story Johnson relies on the works of the imperial secretary Einhard, both his *Life of Charlemagne* and his *Annals*. Agibert notes that Johannes often uses Einhard's words in his memoirs, and this applies particularly to Johannes's description of Charlemagne's appearance—"the words of Einhardus, almost as they are written down in his work about His Grace" (427).

In *The Days of His Grace* Johnson has clearly tried to write if not history at least a historian's novel. This does not of course make it less relevant to the twentieth century. The theme is: how can helpless individuals and peoples preserve any kind of independence, how can they even survive, in the shadow of overwhelming and oppressive power? Writing of Rodgaud's rebellion four years after the crushing of the Hungarian revolt of 1956 Johnson would suggest that the answer lies in a constant awareness of what has happened and is happening. While the concepts of freedom and independence can be preserved there is hope; the oppressors will never sleep easy at nights. The novel itself bears witness to the truth of Johnson's thesis: knowledge of Lombardy and its fate survives into the twentieth century.

III *Ars longa, vita brevis*

Life's Long Day is complementary to *The Days of His Grace*, expressing in concentrated form the story of its more discursive predecessor and expanding and clarifying the ideas. It is according to its subtitle "a novel, told in Rome"—told in a succession of Italian restaurants by The Narrator to a group of friends. The Narrator's story is actually eight stories, set in different periods of time and in different countries, but with a similar theme: a man falls in love with a girl, who disappears. Accompanied by a disreputable servant he pursues her, but falls into a pit. He then rises again to continue his chase.

The first story takes place in the ninth century. Immo, a penniless young fortune-seeker from Saxony, comes to the court of an old friend of his father's—the bishop's court in Chur, Switzerland. Immo is surprisingly singled out to be the husband of the bishop's elder daughter, who is being brought up in the nunnery at Caciae, in the Rhine valley, but when the young man is taken to see his future bride he falls passionately in love with another girl in the nunnery, a girl called Astalda, the illegitimate daughter of a Burgundian countess. With great cunning and deceit Immo manages to return to the nunnery to carry off Astalda, only to elope with the wrong girl. He returns her to the nunnery and she later throws herself into the Rhine.

Stricken with remorse, Immo begins the second story. He enters the monastery of Fulda and his name changes to Donatus. After his own conversion he is anxious to convert others, and he rides out with a troop of soldiers to christianize the heathen in the more distant parts of the Frankish Empire. However, his incessant talk of morality and eternal damnation plagues the soldiers so much that they try to murder him. He escapes from them by tumbling into a hunter's pit, falling on top of a decomposing bear.

A century later Donatus leaves his pit to take part in the third story, which is set in 949 in Pavia, Italy, at the court of King Berengar. Berengar entrusts Donatus with the task of taking a girl called Gisela to Constantinople in payment for a piece of Italy he wants from the Byzantine emperor. Donatus catches a brief glimpse of Gisela, and they immediately recognize one another as Immo and Astalda. The third story merges into the fourth. Donatus is now in Constantinople, but on a second journey, in 968. The

Byzantine emperor has placed him under arrest, and the story is the account of his battle of wits with his jailer. It seems that the girl has disappeared in Greece on the way to Constantinople.

Before Donatus proceeds to Greece he catches a brief glimpse of Astalda in Goslar, Germany, in 1052, at the hanging of a group of Manichaean heretics, which forms the fifth story. The sixth story begins two centuries later, in Genoa in 1272. Donato Guarnerio, a teacher and antiquary, disappears mysteriously from the town with the seventeen-year-old Adala, foster daughter of one of Genoa's leading families. Donato reappears with a degenerate servant in Greece, where he is looking for antiquities to send back to Venice. At Delphi he excavates the statue of a young girl, whom he instantly recognizes; but during the night she disappears. Donato pursues her, but all the information he can get is that she may have been on board a ship that sank off Piraeus.

Another long gap occurs between the sixth and seventh stories. In 1504 Simon de Blonay and Corsant de Bresse joust in Turin to decide the merits, or otherwise, of the married state. The bachelor Corsant loses and rides off with his servant Gabriel to apologize to Madame de Blonay for his doubts about marriage. After a long and roundabout journey, that takes him past the ruins at Caciae, he arrives and duly apologizes. At the same time he sees a girl called Yolande de Villette and immediately falls in love with her. Willing to show in deed what he has already expressed in words he prepares to marry Yolande, but she disappears. The searchers find no trace of her except a line of footprints leading up the slopes of Mont Blanc. The girl reappears in the eighth story in Bordeaux, 1548, as Adèle, the daughter of Tristan de Monneins, the governor. Her lover in this case is René de Bresse, her father's secretary. The governor is murdered by an angry mob protesting against the salt tax, and in reply the Constable of France, Anne de Montmorency, comes to Bordeaux and organizes mass executions. René escapes by hiding in a cellar, where his servant supplies him with food and information. Adèle, he tells him, has again disappeared.

These eight stories are closely interwoven. Often the characters in one particular story are aware of the thoughts and actions of the corresponding characters in the other stories, to the extent of being uncertain as to their own identities, but the most obvious link between the stories is the action that is common to them all. Firstly the lover, whose name may be Immo, Donatus, Corsant, or René, but who is characterized by his loving. His beloved also changes her name, from Astalda to Gisela to Adala to Yolande or Adèle, but she remains constant in her role: being loved, but never attained. The lover is contained during his periods of not loving in some kind of pit, in one case a hunter's pit, in another a prison, but it can be something less obviously constricting: "a hunter's pit of earth or stone, a pit that could be an inn, a monastery, or a town like Constantinople" (145). After a period in this pit, which is also in a sense the grave, the hero rises again to assume another shape in pursuit of a different girl. His servant also comes in various guises. He is the decomposing bear in the hunter's trap, he is the randy monk in the crowd at Goslar. He is not necessarily animal in form; he can be a fallen angel, the hero's guardian angel Gaburiel, a name meant to suggest, presumably, both Gabriel, God's messenger, and Uriel, who answered the questions of Esdras as the jailer in Constantinople answers Donatus's. He can be "a stagnant lake lying in a temporary pit" (8) when he is drunk—which is often—and "he can be likened to an instinct" (7). He represents the less noble features of man, such as gluttony and drunkenness; he complements Donatus as instinct complements love. Astalda, like Donatus, waits in a pit for her resurrection: "in a pit in a forest, in a park, in a castle, behind walls" (234). Her fate is often associated with water: "Once she stood under a waterfall, a torrent of pain; and she was changed when she did so" (14). Her alter ego, the wrong girl, throws herself into the Rhine, and in Caciae she herself falls into a fever: "She lived in her fever, was rocked by its waves, was raised and lowered" (138). As a Grecian statue she vanishes into the Aegean, as Yolande she disappears on a glacier. She is elusive because she is really more a symbol for Donatus's feelings than her own: "Her name was first and foremost 'Longing' " (141)—man's longing, constantly mocked and thwarted.

Naturally Johnson does not perform the feat of linking together eight stories merely as a proof of his technical virtuosity. There is a moral in the story, and Donatus points to it in a document that he addresses from his pit to his beloved, in this case the emperor's daughter Mechtild. His document "can be regarded as a narrator's program and as part of a life chronicle" (143). Firstly, he describes his path to the pit: his overwhelming love for Astalda, his cunning, his remorse, and his arrogant desire to become a saint. He then tells of how he has changed in the pit: "A man is somewhat

changed, perhaps not so much, by lying in a pit like the one just
mentioned. He becomes mild and hard, or seemingly broken; he
follows his own nature and so becomes what he secretly or openly
already is" (144). The lies that have misled him in his dreams of
riches and power are dissipated by the calm reflection that his lengthy
period of meditation gives rise to: he discovers his true nature. This
discovery is assisted by his being freed from the passing of time, for
time has no significance for him during his absence from the surface
of the earth. He can view man's brief life dispassionately and unhur-
riedly:

> What are our life stories concerned with if not with time? With how time
> hastens and pauses? What is our dream, our long dream, if not to be set
> free from time? To be set free from time is, as Rhenus demonstrates, not
> to become free from life but from death. Liberated, that is all. Only trans-
> ferred from bad life to good life, but liberated from death. We grasp the
> days, hold them as we can hold on to days, let them go as we are forced to
> let them go—we are abandoned by them. But we do not lose them when
> our grip relaxes. They remain, and yet we are free of them, if we have the
> right will, the right state of mind. Let them go and still have them. That
> was my feeling when I stepped out of the recently mentioned pit.
>
> (146–47)

Donatus urges man to live each day to the full. He repeats the
words of Horace that Immo uses when he abandons his hopes of
an ultimately advantageous marriage in favor of immediate happiness with Astalda: "*Carpe diem!* Be present! Use the time you
are present in! Grasp every day and let it fall!" (147). Even the imprisoned Donatus in Constantinople echoes this cry: "Sometimes
I remembered the poet Horace's good and helpless words: 'Grasp
the day!' And I grasped the days and nights of starvation, the only
ones of living time there were to grasp" (209). The days so grasped
must disappear into the past, but they can remain in memory. As
memories they may cause pain and distress, as they often do in
Johnson's novels, as they do here when Immo flees from Caciae.
But with "the right state of mind," the state of mind that can view
memories clarified of their grief, then "they remain, and yet we are
free of them." Johannes Lupigis is an example.

What applies to individual human lives applies to human life
in general. Although the individual dies he lives on in other men in
the future, just as he incorporates in his life elements from previous

human lives: "Men die, man lives eternally. Through man, men always survive the Day of Judgment" (147). This is the justification of the linking of the eight stories in the novel. Each separate incarnation of the lover dies—but the lover lives on. Time may be a straight line divided by the present moment into past and future, but this mathematical representation does not correspond to human experience. Rhenus, the River Rhine, is the symbol for time in *Life's Long Day*. Time sweeps away all earthly things. As Donatus puts it in his Byzantine prison: "I heard a mighty river and saw remnants of life floating away on a black surface with white foam. I saw towns floating away. I felt the river was Rhenus" (209). But the river does not carry its prey into oblivion. Donatus declares from his pit: "I do not count the days any longer, and sometimes I have felt freed from time. Freed as a river can be, rich in time and freed from time, like the winding Rhenus. Yes, like Rhenus, where the past runs into the present and the present mixes with a past that in this way continues to live. Let me put it like this: a river where many ages flow abreast" (145–46).

When Donatus is freed from time he is "transferred from bad life to good life." He rejects his earlier dreams of power and his subsequent religious fanaticism: "Despite my sometimes hard temperament in the past I became on the whole mild in the pit, though not all the time. I venture to say that I revealed a certain talent for mildness, though not a mildness of the yielding kind, as some may be tempted to believe by misinterpreting my behavior. I became more clearly aware that the evil that exists in men ought not to be belittled or underestimated by the observer. . . . But I also became more clearly aware that the good that men can display ought not to be underestimated either" (144–45). Donatus develops a deep hatred of inhumanity and tyranny which, like Johannes Lupigis, he conceals beneath a mild exterior. He can smile obligingly when he dines with Emperor Nicephorus in Constantinople or drinks with Berengar in Pavia, but he is always aware of what they represent: the evils of power.

Ultimately there cannot be masters and servants, jailers and prisoners, for all men are members one of another—"We are *also* others" (148). A particular illustration of this is provided by the struggle between Donatus and his jailer in Constantinople. Their positions of prisoner and guard change constantly as first one then the other gets the upper hand. Donatus compares the jailer to

John the Baptist and Judas Iscariot and himself takes Christ's
words into his mouth (190 & 201), but their theological relationship
changes too, as the jailer adopts the pose of Christ suffering on the
cross (207). Their roles are interchangeable; they are man.

The document Donatus despatches from his pit is also "a narrator's program." For as well as being a lover Donatus is a narrator,
concerned with describing his search for the beloved and posing
questions about life and time: "I am the servant of the questions,
I produce them as pictures, as voices, as shapes, as assertions"
(147). He dreams of "a fertility of words" (143)—the words he
scatters round him will carry his experiences and his ideas into the
future, as his roots suck up nourishment from the past. The symbol
of the narrator in this novel is a blade of grass on a distant shore,
a plant that survives all catastrophes, seeds itself, renews itself,
listening to voices from the past and whispering words to the future.
A final refinement of the story is that The Narrator himself seems
to be a reincarnation of Donatus. At the end of the novel he catches
sight of his hero and heroine, and he sees himself: "I saw myself
as in a trembling mirror, not the mirroring of a water's surface,
but a mirror with uneven, dusty-misted glass. Yet the woman was
not Caroline [his wife] but another I had lost long ago and whose
name I had forgotten" (325). That narrators use themselves as
material for their books is a point repeatedly made in the novel;
in particular, the French chronicler Froissart is cited as "a typical
narrator" (320), a man living with the very material he is describing.

In a postscript to *Life's Long Day* Johnson writes that it is not
to be regarded as a historical novel, although it mentions names
and events that are recorded in historical documents. The difference
between literature and history is brought out in discussions between
The Narrator and one of his audience, The Historian.[7] When The
Historian protests at The Narrator's cavalier treatment of historical
fact, the latter replies: "History is lived. I am trying to say how it
can be experienced afterwards by eyes staring into books, by ears
catching the whisperings between the words" (244). The author's
interpretations must begin where the historian's researches end.
The author is presented with his historical material and he then tries
to bring it to life. If necessary, he will go beyond the limits of the
historian's knowledge; in connection with the executions at Goslar
The Historian points out how little they know about the life of the
chronicler-monk who described the hangings, but The Narrator

cheerfully tries to psychoanalyze him (231). While the historian must stick to fact, the author can employ "crude distortions in what he considers to be the right direction, obvious lies to extract truths, even falsification of the truth to direct attention to it" (135). Both author and historian are trying to understand what man is like and why he does what he does, but while the historian, with his objective approach, can build on previous results, the author is trying to give an individual interpretation of the past, and since time is limited he must do it intuitively, through literature. As The Historian says: "The incredible is an excellent means of approaching the probable" (301). But of course it is only "the probable" an author can hope to attain; he cannot in the end say "what it was *really* like." The Narrator is forced to admit that literature is mostly a diversion: "Even the most horrible poem is a diversion in comparison with only slightly embittered, faintly pungent reality" (301). And with devastating consistency he describes Montmorency's bloodbath in Bordeaux in 1548 as "an entertainment" (303).

The Narrator takes considerable liberties with his historical sources. Sometimes he builds up a whole scene from just a few lines of documentation, as in the case of the executions at Goslar, which merit only a brief mention in the chronicle of Hermann Contractus.[8] He then places Donatus on the scene, though he is nowhere mentioned in the chronicle. Similarly, fictitious accounts of Donato Guarnerio are inserted into extensive and genuine quotations from the annals of Genoa.[9] The Narrator can also confuse his historical sources as he confuses his stories. Donatus's mission from Berengar's court and his imprisonment in Constantinople are based on the two separate Byzantine missions of Liudprand, Bishop of Cremona, the first being described in his *Antapodosis,* the second in *The Embassy to Constantinople.*[10] In his account of the banquet Donatus attends on his release, The Narrator freely mixes incidents from the two journeys. In one case The Narrator appropriates a preface but ignores the book it introduces: the letter Donatus prepares in his pit is ostensibly addressed to Mechtild, Abbess of Quedlinburg—a dedication that is taken from Widukind's *Saxon Histories.*[11]

Donatus and Astalda are developed from ideas in *The Days of His Grace,* from the monk Meldebrand who rides with Conald's troops (401–402) and from Angila's illegitimate daughter Radberta (335). However, Johnson's use of history is clearly very different in the two books. In *The Days of His Grace* he cuts lengthwise, along the river of time, while in *Life's Long Day* he cuts breadthwise, across the river where all ages flow abreast. Time stands still; the unchanging pattern of life is revealed beneath the differences in its temporary manifestations. The Narrator is also caught in that pattern, both as a man and as an author. The story he tells is older than he is and will outlive him: he is only its momentary servant. As his part in the story comes to an end he sees the characters ride out of his life:

They abandoned him. They took part of his own life with them. They would continue to move in the directions of their own lives, lose one another and be separated again, vanish. They would be rediscovered by someone wanting to see their faces, be sought life's long day by someone not this narrator, but a younger, a new narrator. This narrator too would become silent, step aside, let the story wander on its way to narrators far ahead in time, when this age's narrator, when the narrators of many ages, would long since be dumb and vanished and all their words only whisperings of a seeding grass on a distant coast.   (329–30)

CHAPTER 8

Europe and Idealism

I Put Away the Sun

TWO novels remain to be discussed: *Lägg undan solen* (*Put Away the Sun*, 1951) and *Favel ensam* (*Favel Alone*, 1968). These books are very much in the tradition of the prewar Mårten Torpare novels; that is, they are comments on contemporary problems and ideas. While they do not represent Johnson at his best, they are interesting for the light they throw on the techniques and ideas behind his more substantial historical novels.

Put Away the Sun presents a cross-section of life in twentieth-century Europe, where men have been caught in political cross-currents, revolutions, and two catastrophic wars: "No one has emerged unscathed from these five decades" (64). The action, such as it is, takes place on a mountain in the Alps, between two republics, round about the year 1950. There have just been coups-d'état in the two republics, and refugees fleeing from one or other of the new regimes gather in a hut on the top of the boundary mountain. The mountain is temporarily no-man's land, but its potential mineral wealth—uranium—ensures that it will soon be fought over. The refugees have one day to sleep and collect their thoughts and strength and the following night they can escape to a third country. The book is principally a study of the lives of these refugees, who stand for so many other Europeans with equally tragic fates.

The story is seen largely through the eyes of an Englishman with the international name of Henry Templeman Crofter Brace, "Crofter" being incidentally the English for *Torpare*.[1] Crofter Brace is the dramatic critic of a London newspaper and he comments on the events he witnesses as though they were part of a play and as though the participants were acting them out. But Crofter Brace is also a politician and a European, and he is deeply involved in what is happening, if only as an observer: "He was very aware, the intellectual in the prison of political events, the kind who may be the last European. He couldn't help seeing and hearing and he knew it was suicide to ignore things" (68). When Crofter Brace comes to define what he means by European he takes Churchill as an example, with his "common sense and passion" (95): "What is it that makes me a European—if I am one? A certain amount of reason, which isn't cold as ice. Ice-cold reason is a phrase. There's no reason without some measure of passion. . . . The desire to analyze things is also passion" (96). It is this passion that draws Crofter Brace away from London and Kate, his lady friend, to the mountain hut and the possibility of never returning. He cannot even play an active role when he is there; he is "a listening post" (75): "He was powerless now and could not influence events, in any case not noticeably. His task must be limited to observing them" (154).

The characters Crofter Brace observes on his self-imposed mission are of several kinds. There are three revolutionaries: Biller, Gallo, and Paul. Their different approaches to revolution are summed up in their pamphlets on "the way of necessary force, or the way of dangerous force, or the way between what is soothing and pacifying and what is hard and necessarily and mercilessly fatal" (243). Biller is the realist who prides himself on his unsentimentality. The end, he feels, justifies the means, and the means must be purges and mass executions. His opposite is Gallo, who believes in bloodless revolution, while Paul, who appears only as a corpse in the novel, wavers between the two. The book is principally concerned with Gallo. He represents the pacifist philosophy, similar to Krapotkin's, that lies behind so much of the thought in Johnson's works, and he represents it at the end of the road. Gallo has devoted his life to preaching the need for revolution: "Not crude revolution, with killing and exterminating, but Krapotkin's, with enlightenment, the spreading of light, a belief in goodness" (173). At one point he actually obtained power but he failed to destroy his opponents and was soon ousted in a counter-coup. He fled, leaving behind his wife and children. He sees this flight as a terrible personal sacrifice, while the other characters in the book see it as a cowardly escape. Despite his grief Gallo has continued his activities, plotting and lecturing, but he begins to feel his message is no longer getting across. His audiences are the old faithful; the young are not interested: "Before, he felt impotently, the same manuscript had been an attack with irony in its tone. Now it was defense: a man stepping backwards and waving his arms so as not to lose his balance. 'We must take the line we've always taken,' he said, 'no aid to militarism, to dictatorship. I'm aware that we may have to use weapons to save our possibilities of surviving and attaining an era without weapons. But our goal must, *must* be to abolish weapons'" (197). When Gallo is forced to flee a second time, up to the mountain hut, he realizes he can go no further. When the other refugees leave the hut he refuses to accompany them: "We can't cope with what we have in front of us. . . . Perhaps we can cope with what we have behind us, presumably we get used to it. But it's different with what we have in front of us" (296).

Closely connected with the three revolutionaries is a middle-aged woman called Gina. Outwardly she is hard, but she is driven by intense sexual passion and perhaps by hate too. She has spent some time before the war in a concentration camp with her baby daughter, and when she escaped temporarily to be with her lover—Paul—she was unable to return and had to abandon her child. Since then she has been actively engaged in revolutionary activities. One of her former lovers is also present in the hut—Eugenio, a man of quite a different character from the revolutionaries. His occupation is smuggling and he comes of a family of bandits: one of his brothers has emigrated to the United States and duly ended his days in the electric chair, while another has been killed nearer home in a battle with customs guards. Yet in the end it is the down-to-earth bandit, not the idealists, who saves the refugees, leading them across the landslip that blocks their escape route from the hut. Eugenio is accompanied by a woman called Caterina, whose warmth and softness inspire Crofter Brace to see her as a symbol of "all the women of mankind in all ages" (312). A young couple complete the numbers of those in the hut; they are Jules and his girl friend Silvia, of whom Crofter Brace observes: "She was most of all, however unplayable her role might seem to be, she was most of all mankind's future" (148). Jules turns out to be Gallo's son, while Silvia is the daughter Gina had abandoned in the concentration camp. Both are understandably distrustful of idealists. The complicated interrelationships between the characters in the book are scarcely accidental. They are meant to underline Crofter Brace's thesis that "everybody's fate has points of contact with everybody else's" (5).[2]

There is a symbolism behind the realistic story in the novel. For example, the characters are on a political frontier, but they also use the word "frontier" in more abstract ways. Gallo, who has reached the limits of his endurance, says: "We are *on* the frontier.

That means we're between two frontiers. And no one knows where
the real frontier runs at the moment, since it hasn't been drawn yet.
We are rounded up by and inside a frontier, tied up by a frontier
as by a rope. Call it a noose if you like" (34). Gallo also uses the
word "frontier" when he describes his first flight twenty years
previously: "Perhaps he tried to reach the frontiers, reach out to
the frontiers and beyond the frontiers. . . . The frontiers of everything. . . . Or the frontiers of his own possibilities. Man's. Life's"
(50). He cannot repeat this attempt to be greater than his fate; now
the frontier ensnares him. Eugenio proposes a solution that is
neither superhuman nor despairing, but realistic: "You can go
along *the frontier* if you have the right kind of understanding and
know something about the mountains" (279). Idealism has to be
sacrificed to the demands of mere survival, a delicate balancing act
between two dangers.

Another symbol, which is closely associated with that of frontiers,
is the landslide or avalanche. Gallo describes the disaster that swept
away his family as an avalanche (188). In the lecture he delivers to
the faithful he replaces his former symbol of hope, "the old image
of the sun finally rising out of a misty sea" (198), by the picture of a
man who loses his wife and children in an avalanche: "but he kept
on working for the cause and didn't stop hoping in mankind, in
knowledge, in science's possibilities for good. . ." (199). Now he
faces a real mountain in movement, for the escape route is blocked
by a landslip; as Crofter Brace prophetically notes of Gallo at the beginning of the novel: "Just now he looked like a man without means
of retreat in front of a landslip" (28). Gallo refuses to face a second
avalanche and stays in the hut; and when Gina and Biller try to
escape they are crushed by a landslide. The landslide is in one sense
a symbol of men's passions and the lack of control that there exists
over them when they are aroused. When Crofter Brace returns to
London he tells Kate about avalanches:

"They roll," he said. "They rumble and thunder and reverberate. They
sweep down the mountain, blindly it seems, and they say 'Whoosh!' They
follow certain channels, certain furrows in the mountain, and doubtless
they have a kind of sense of their goal, in spite of everything. *But they know
nothing else about their path, they merely follow it, they are nothing—they
are the avalanche.*"
    "Are you talking about them or the avalanche now, Henry?"
    "About them," he said.   (311)

It is only poetic justice that the revolutionaries should be swept away by the forces they set in motion. But the other characters can cross with Eugenio's help, and in contrast to the political idealists, who have abandoned their followers and relations when things have become too dangerous, Eugenio risks his life to save them.

There are other symbols in the novel, but they are of minor or even obscure significance. There is the rising sun, Gallo's old symbol of hope. Now he cries: "If only they could put away the damned sun so that I can sleep at last" (295). But the sun rises to shine on those who escape as they enter a new day in freedom. Other symbols include the mountain—treacherous with its avalanches and its explosive contents—and water, which seems to represent life, reinvigoration. However, these symbols, and the symbolical significance that the author sometimes lends other natural objects in his descriptions of the scenery, seem too diffuse and unorganized to allow a strictly symbolic interpretation of the novel. They emphasize the theme rather than deepen it.

A further dimension is added to the book by history. Both Gallo and Gina are aware that they are repeating a sequence of events that occurred in a slave revolt in Ancient Rome. Gallo has taken his name after the leader of this revolt—Gallus. A further refinement of the historical parallelism is that Crofter Brace, who sees it all as scenes in a play, has recently seen and reviewed a play about this slave revolt. Both the play and the slave revolt appear to be Johnson's invention, though an obvious source for the invention is provided by the Spartacists in Germany (1917–19), who took their name from the slave leader Spartacus in Ancient Rome. Gallo himself throws doubt on his predecessor's existence: "It's a fantasy, a dream that may not be in Gibbon, an embroidery on history" (147). Like Gallo, Gallus has deserted his followers, but he has finally been crucified. When Gallo is aware of the past he is also aware of his namesake's fate. Crofter Brace points out the disadvantages of such a historical sense, when both past and present are simultaneously present in men's minds: "This simultaneity is the dread of our time, or the source of it, the dread caused by the possibility of quick comparisons. Dread and joy, comedy and tragedy, pain and pleasure, death, birth, death again, rebirth—in our consciousness the past and present are there beside each other" (55). This concept of simultaneity is fully exploited in *Life's Long Day*; in *Put Away the Sun* it is still only a suggestion in the background.

Put Away the Sun is on the whole a rather too discursive novel, leaving no very firm impression behind. The characters in the hut engage in desultory and disjointed conversation, apparently to little purpose. What most survives is the section entitled "The Stories," consisting of five short stories that describe the lives of some of the characters. Particularly entertaining are those of Gina and Eugenio. Gina's stay in the concentration camp and her escape is told to the accompaniment of a crude folk song; while the disreputable career of Eugenio and his brothers is told in terms of noble sentiment, grave injustice, and aggrieved innocence.

II Favel Alone

Favel Alone has much in common with *Put Away the Sun*. The surface action is largely concentrated within a few hours, which are devoted to discussion, but the story also delves deeply into the past, where the important action has taken place. *Favel Alone* is a book about Europe, about idealists and idealism, and like *Put Away the Sun* it makes frequent use of symbols to express abstract ideas and emotions. The basic plot is sketchy: In the late 1960s Peter Favel-Hyth comes to the town of Woodham, Buckinghamshire (which can be identified by its pubs as Amersham, 25 miles northwest of London),[3] to call on a young couple called Martin and Miriam and possibly to meet his old friend Dr. Charlon-Loday. All four characters are refugees from Nazi Germany. Favel-Hyth wants to discuss the past with them. In particular, he wants to tell Martin and Miriam that he is in fact Miriam's father and that her mother and her legal father were betrayed to the Nazis by Martin's father, who was Charlon-Loday's son Paul. On his way to talk to Martin and Miriam, Favel-Hyth meets Charlon-Loday engaged in clipping a hedge. The core of the novel consists of a discussion between Favel-Hyth and Charlon-Loday, perched at the top of a ladder. After the discussion Favel-Hyth sets off to call on Martin and Miriam, but no one answers the door and he leaves without meeting them.

The long scene between Favel-Hyth and Charlon-Loday is described through Favel-Hyth's eyes. Charlon-Loday is seen from the outside only. Favel is sixty-five years old, a writer, a "professional spectator and narrator" (7). He is of German origin, British by nationality, and resident in Rome: he is a European.

As a European he has experienced in full the catastrophe that has overwhelmed the continent in the twentieth century: "a fatherland in times and regions that burst into a thousand pieces" (225). In the late 1960s he spends a couple of months on vacation in Denmark and he finds himself face to face with his past: "Sometimes it seemed to him it was only now he had seriously begun to investigate P. Favel-Hyth's real experiences, or at any rate the results of what he had experienced. He was often worried, indeed several times very disturbed, by memories that came and brushed against him" (7–8). He decides that perhaps he can come to terms with these memories now, and he sets off for Berlin. There he relives the scene from 1934 in which Miriam's parents were removed by the secret police. This is a scene that recurs throughout *Favel Alone,* a scene of horror balanced by another, pleasanter, recurrent memory, of a vacation by the sea in Norway, when Miriam was conceived. Prompted by his memories of Berlin Favel comes to Woodham to tell Martin and Miriam about the past and to achieve clarity in his own mind with a view to writing about it all. The past is still very much part of his present, as it so often is in Johnson's novels, and for Favel it is a struggle to come to terms with it. He has suffered both personal misfortunes and the general misfortune that has struck him as a European idealist: the misfortune of seeing ideals shattered, of seeing revolutions turn to bloodbaths:

He sought old methods for overcoming the memories, hindering the movements of the past, winning a calm tempo in his existence in the present, controlling the flight and course of time. He did what a reasonable man should do when he realizes his own despair inside himself and the despair that streams towards him from the world outside to become his despair as well. It was that kind of despair he was exposed to. The methods of escape he employed were attempts to control the changes and the lack of change at the same time. That means to be borne or to sail or hover on the winds of change and make one's way through the temporary lull of existence, the immobile memories, their petrified mass.   (219–20)

Charlon-Loday has been more successful at overcoming the past than Favel has. He has seen even more of the horror of twentieth-century Europe, for he is older, and he describes it in detail for Favel, as material for his writing. Yet despite his revolutionary involvement Charlon has remained "our age's reasonably guiltless man" (55). And he has not been crushed by his disappointments. He is "a calm observer with fair hopes, at once innocent, childlike, and trusting; and very experienced" (83). "Charlon's eyes were light blue, as before, and as before very clear: no traces of the aching smoke from the world's conflagrations or of salt tears unsuited to the whites of those eyes. Charlon-Loday still looked very much like himself" (56). Charlon has been a doctor of medicine but he has found it as important to patch up people's souls as their bodies. He becomes: "A man sticking together people and life itself and what is known as Development when it had gotten a scratch and Progress when it began to limp with its right or its left foot and when it was a matter of finding medicines against Reaction. All the time it was a question of somehow helping to repair people and ideologies that had gone wrong or were in the process of breaking down or had some pain somewhere" (169–70). Now in his retirement he devotes himself to hedges, which become for him a symbol of escapism with their "suitability as a means of escape" (66). But despite Charlon's fatherly care hedges are a dwindling protection: "The hedges are kept at the height and width they are used to, naturally. But they're not so dense now" (63). Charlon himself stands high above the hedges on his ladder, "a ladder that gave a good view with the possibility of even wider areas of vision" (84), but not all can face the world as he does; they need the protection hedges afford. Consequently he advises Favel not to burden Martin and Miriam with his problems. When it becomes clear that Favel is determined to visit them, Charlon begs him to tell them encouraging things about the future, to give them fresh courage: "Let them remain young. Lie as best you can. They won't be able to cope with all truths" (173). Charlon wonders if Favel isn't really *exploiting* Martin's and Miriam's position because as an author he finds it interesting, and Favel himself begins to feel that they do not need the clarity he has come to give them: "Clarity is a demand of many philosophers, but most people call for happiness, peace, ordinary quiet and excitement—not clarity. . . . Can *they* live without clarity? It's probably without it, because of a lack of it, that they can live" (215–16). Favel must renounce his parental claims on Miriam and he must remain alone in the world, alone with his own problems. He must model himself on Charlon, who has discovered that the "life lie," deception practiced out of kindness, is more important than abstract and harmful truth; on Charlon who can face his past with equanimity: "Charlon distanced himself from his answers and yet answered with clarity. He turned away, looked into the realm of the birds, and said loudly, clearly, or in a mumble that was more than clear, that he knew all that about Paul, that he had known it for many years. Charlon rests in the evenings, looks forward to the days to come" (217).

Favel not only struggles with his memories; he is also beset by political doubts. He has seen too many idealists in action in Europe, and their behavior has led him to question the value of idealism: the concept seems to have been devalued by the crimes committed in its name. Favel recalls a Ukrainian refugee who had experienced bloody revolution at first hand, and who was forced to consider whether both executioners and martyrs killed and died less for ideals than for the desire to be noticed and admired. Charlon rubs in Favel's doubt by laying great stress on the fact that the Nazis thought they were taking part in the creation of the ideal state; and he points to less dramatic instances of idealists who become good bureaucrats and continue to profess ideals while acting against them: where their ideals put out proudly to sea, only a blanket of mist remains (158).

But the behavior of individual idealists does not mean that idealism is a bad thing. Charlon's final message in the novel seems to be "that we cannot get along without a Utopia—a country that doesn't exist anywhere, an island shaped like a crescent moon, in a sea that doesn't exist, an absolutely essential island for a humanity that doesn't want to perish" (246–47). The mention of Utopia is a reminder of a historical illustration of the problems of Favel and Charlon. *Utopia* is Sir Thomas More's account of the island where everything is perfect—an island supposedly discovered by a sailor called Raphael Hythloday, whose name is divided between Favel and Charlon. Throughout *Favel Alone* both Favel and Charlon mention More's name and his book. More is there in the background much as Gallus is in *Put Away the Sun,* though not so much as a warning as the ideal of the idealist: the chancellor to Henry VIII who in obedience to his religious ideals first resigned his office and then went to the block.

Favel Alone is a novel about ideals and political engagement, but Johnson is particularly concerned to defend art from the compulsion to be "committed." Charlon is, among other things, an artist, and he reacts negatively when Favel attempts to read a political message into some of his pictures: "They were not committed other than that they were held together by *Gefühle*—a feeling for collections of color executed according to the methods of the time, combinations of color I felt a strong desire to create" (104). He dismisses commitment in art as the attempt to stuff "something *that looks like passion* into the sausage skin of an art form" (104). Interpretations of his art are the responsibility not of the artist but the spectator. Art can of course help men to understand their own problems better if they can project them into a work of art. This is what Favel does with Charlon's paintings, depicting the Elizabethan interiors of Woodham's pubs. Staring into these pictures, as into a closed room, Favel sees a self-satisfied, well-fed, welfare state: "There was security there, but I don't remember wanting any of that kind of security. There was the horror of security, the stuffiness" (99). The word Favel thinks best describes the sensation he detects in the pictures is "weariness": "Weariness with all the so-called ordered existence we had gotten here or in other places after the war, whether it was an ordered struggle for existence or a welfare-state existence ordered in the best possible way in a reasonably pleasant society, for example the only slightly flawed, somewhat cracked society of England. Weariness with the worlds of reality and illusion—I don't know what, but deep weariness and a powerful longing for something beautiful but difficult to describe, something—well, almost incomprehensible fantasies about everything that words can scarcely grasp and display and extend to us" (100–101). The longing that Favel sees in these pictures seems to be related to Gallo's wish to reach and pass beyond the frontiers of his world. The idea is no more explained in *Favel Alone* than it is in *Put Away the Sun*. It is the merest suggestion in the background. What dominates the novels is the basic need to survive and function, even if it be by dubious stratagems or in doubtful company—such as Eugenio—or on a diet of half-truths and concealment, as in *Favel Alone*.

CHAPTER 9

Conclusion

I *The Storyteller*

Y ES—oh yes—the novel tells a story," says E. M. Forster regretfully, noting that the novelist must work within the constricting tradition of the oral storyteller.[1] If the narrator cannot keep his audience in some sort of suspense, he will send them to sleep, whether they be Neanderthal men squatting round the camp fire or twentieth-century intellectuals in centrally heated libraries. Yet the story will be at best irrelevant and at worst antagonistic to the real aims of the novelist of ideas, who is anxious to lay bare the basic patterns of human existence. The accidents of circumstance—time, place, action—conceal rather than reveal the fundamental nature of man's inward life and the ideas and passions that drive him. Not surprisingly, then, Johnson's novels suggest an author who is impatient with the need to provide a story. Johnson is not a great inventor of high adventure or a master of complicated intrigue. Sometimes he attempts to do away with the story altogether and to substitute discussion and analysis for it, as in *Put Away the Sun,* or *Romantic Tale* and *The Course of Time;* and though the audience nowadays may not kill the narrator who fails to keep them entertained, at least they consign his books to second-hand bookshops, where these three works are easy to find. Johnson is really at his best when he has some basic story and elaborates it: his own life, in *The Novel About Olof;* political events, in *Krilon;* someone else's story, in *The Swell on the Beaches;* historical fact, as in *Dreams of Roses and Fire.* Given a story, he will tell it with all the imagination and ingenuity he possesses. But his heart is not in the business of incident and excitement; the real action is elsewhere.

A story is a sequence of events in time; yet the steady progression of happenings has little to do with inner time, psychological time. Some moments appear to be longer than others. Time can stand still for Odysseus on Calypso's isle, in a life where the sequence of events does not imply progression—and then seven years can

143

roll over him in a fraction of a second. Moreover, events may be ordered very differently in man's consciousness than they are in time. They may, in memory, be thoroughly shuffled, or they may all be there simultaneously, time past and time future all contained in time present. Such quirks of the human experience of time are Johnson's special interest, and in *Put Away the Sun* he lets Crofter Brace discuss the esthetic problems involved:

> I am *here*—but all the same I am *there*. How does that figure? The necessary simultaneity, the impression of being present everywhere in time and space, cannot be created in literature, but only in pictorial art. Painters, artists, can give us *then* and *now* and far and near in one canvas, one picture. Writers cannot succeed in this, for however fragmented and transposed events may be shown, one word has to follow another, the picture that the words give glides, sweeps, moves in lines passing from now to then and from then to now and between far and near, between the particular and the general.   (54–55)

Much of the intricate construction in Johnson's novels has to do with his attempts to escape the tyranny of time and ordering. Memories expand, if not to Proustian proportions, at least, in *Krilon,* to the size of short stories. The time sequence can be thoroughly shaken up, as in *The Clouds over Metapontion;*[2] while in *Life's Long Day,* "all ages flow abreast." By these means Johnson hopes to create in the audience's mind a brief sensation of simultaneity. In the end, of course, the story will sabotage the impressions, and the tidy human mind will disentangle the muddle and sort it into the inexorable movement of events from beginning to end.

Another disadvantage of the story is that it may distract attention from more important matters. The particular incidents in a story and the individual peculiarities of its characters can be the trees that obscure the outlines of the forest. Johnson usually places a certain distance between himself and his story: a well-developed irony keeps the characters in their place, or they suddenly contract into figures in a historical perspective. In history especially, Johnson seems to find the distance that suits his art:

> If you peel away the historical trappings from, let us say, a twelfth-century lord of the manor, you will find that as far as absolute authority is concerned he is not all that different from a modern office tyrant (and

those who work in offices know that there are plenty of despots there). But it is a laborious business writing about all a clerk's trivialities to show him up as a despot. It's easier, and quicker, to deck him out as a lord instead—and it is also more rewarding from the artistic point of view.[3]

A comparison of the two parts of *The Clouds over Metapontion* reveals exactly what Johnson means.

If the story is a regrettable but necessary survival from prehistoric times, what about the storyteller? His ancestor sat three-dimensionally in front of the camp fire and spoke to his unsophisticated Neanderthal contemporaries. The role of storyteller in these more disembodied and intellectual days is one Johnson adopts rather self-consciously. Two examples of traditional storytelling occur in his works: Odysseus talking to the Phaeacians, and Anselm recounting episodes from Lombard history in Forojuli. In both cases Johnson stands outside the magic circle of speaker and audience. He is busy explaining what really happened to Odysseus and why he is describing it as he is, or he is Johannes Lupigis admiring the way his uncle is manipulating the audience. Johnson similarly watches his own efforts to tell his story.

Firstly, Johnson the storyteller is uneasy about his place in the novel: "You try to narrate something as though you weren't involved in the narrative; you call yourself—an eye. But where is the eye, this strange, seeing eye without a body?" he asks in *Life's Long Day* (129). He can hide behind a character who is himself a narrator, or he may be honest and place himself fairly and squarely in the story as "the re-narrator" (*Krilon*), or "I" (*Dreams of Roses and Fire*), or as an actual character telling the story, "The Narrator" (*Life's Long Day*); and then he is back to the point of watching himself tell the story.

Johnson worries not only about his physical position in the story, but also about his position between the reader and reality.[4] He must inevitably give a subjective impression of what is happening: "This is how I tell the story; in actual fact it is different," as he puts it in *Krilon's Journey* (311). Similar reservations apply to the subsidiary narrators in the novels: Henrik Fax in *Rain at Dawn,* or Themistogenes in *The Clouds over Metapontion,* who says: "My personality is a mirror, it has a frame; consequently, its possibilities are limited, and the picture is also dependent on the light and shade in my mind" (190). The storyteller cannot encompass reality, though he can make his story as comprehensive as possible, as in *Krilon,* or he can introduce several narrators and so several subjective but different points of view into a novel, as in *Dreams of Roses and Fire.* In the end, though, a story must reveal more about its author than about reality: "Is there anyone who knows the reality of the world or the reality of the village at this moment? Is it not rather a story of what the storyteller believes reality and the present to be, and so a story about the storyteller himself— like most stories" (*Traces past Colonos,* 311).

The storyteller forms a subjective picture of reality: how is he to convey this picture to his audience? Not, it appears from the discussions in *Krilon* (see Chapter 5, above), by describing exactly what he sees. He may have to distort or falsify what he sees as the truth, in order to convey its nature to other people, or he may have to disguise it in a fairy tale, like Odysseus. In his attempts to convey to others "what it was really like" Johnson is in a direct line of descent from his Neanderthal ancestor—but in his constant preoccupation with his attempts to convey "what it was really like," he attains a sophistication that threatens to obscure the actual business of storytelling.

II *The Novelist*

The novelist does rather more than tell a story: he expresses, if only by implication, some attitude to life, and it is this that attracts or repels readers. Johnson's work is characterized at its best by a sense of tension. Like Odysseus on his raft, man is continually threatened by powers that may overwhelm him; he lives on the world of the aspen leaf, where even the aged Agibert, secure in his monastery library, can write: "I am seeking. What? I don't know, perhaps eternal peace. I know I shall not attain it while I am alive" (*The Days of His Grace,* 185). Man maintains his precarious balance by exerting opposing forces against those acting on him, by pitting indifference against engagement, skepticism against passion, mildness against anger. He rests in unstable equilibrium somewhere in the calm at the center of the storm.

Such tension exists on several levels in Johnson's works. It is obvious in his characters: Andersson in *Town in Darkness* fights against hopeless disappointment with a cynical smile; Clerk in *Remembering* suppresses passionate love with emotional frigidity;

Olle Oper in *Romantic Tale* uses language as a weapon: "The stilted language that came close to officialese was excellent: a fence that prevented one from tumbling—blind with emotion, upset, furious, hurt—down into sentimentality" (325); Odysseus controls his feelings on leaving Calypso and on meeting Penelope with elaborate phrases; Johannes Lupigis wears a "well-practiced smile" and uses irony to balance his hatred of Charlemagne. The control of despair is a major theme in Johnson's works. Characters who cannot place restraints on their emotions and so tumble headlong into sentimentality and self-pity are the natural prey of the Devil: "What is evil? What cannot a man be driven to by sickness, grief, disappointment, or lust for power!" Donatus exclaims (*Life's Long Day,* 144). But the character who grapples hopefully with despair, whose faith is tempered by skepticism and who fights with dispassionate fervor—he is the hero of Johnson's novels, and one of his names is Johannes Krilon.

It is not only the characters who exist in a state of tension. The content of Johnson's novels is checked by the method of expression. In *Life's Long Day* there is a comment on Montaigne, prince of skeptics, that could equally apply to Johnson: "What is the skepticism that is a mixture of respect, *fierce* irony, and deep anger, all expressed in mild words?" (306). In his early works, such as *Commentary on a Falling Star,* Johnson counteracts the catastrophes and the injustices in his stories with a cynical exuberance of style. Later the expressions become milder. In *The Novel About Olof* and *Krilon* grim reality is balanced by the grace or absurdity of the fairy tale; in *Life's Long Day* Montmorency's bloodbath is described as "an entertainment." Mild words, deliberately drained of emotion, form the language of most of Johnson's recent work. Some readers, consequently, find Johnson too cerebral and detached, but this is to misunderstand the way the novels work. The emotion is in the subject matter; the style counteracts the emotion; and the reader stands in between, at the point of balance.

Johnson is recognizably in a European tradition, both in his humanism and his art. He is also, by European standards, an outstanding novelist, robbed of world fame by the not widely read language that is his mother tongue. International fame has descended rather capriciously on Scandinavian authors in the past, and Johnson's works may never be widely known outside a small circle of Scandinavian readers. To those who can understand him he presents what he considers to be essentials: "Man's greatness and the fear of his being degraded. Children's games and seriousness. Unhappiness and joy. Despair and consolation. The course of time: to view it with as undistracted a gaze as possible" (*The Course of Time,* 424). Johnson's art is to be found at the still but unstable center of the turning world, and there it is unsurpassed.

Notes and References

Chapter One

1. For Johnson's ancestry see "Möten," *SLT*, XXIX (1966), 4–6.
2. "Optimism—eller vad?" *Hågkomster och livsintryck*, XIII (Uppsala, 1932), p. 270.
3. *Ibid.*, p. 272.
4. See Örjan Lindberger, "'Enligt uppfattning.' Om en roman av Eyvind Johnson och några protokollsböcker," *Nordisk tidskrift*, XXXIII (1957), 197–207.
5. See an unpublished *trebetygsuppsats* in Humanistiska biblioteket, University of Stockholm: Åke Nordin, "Eyvind Ung. Några drag i Eyvind Johnsons diktning mot bakgrunden av hans tidigare utvecklingshistoria," (University of Stockholm, 1945). Johnson's poems are collected in a supplement to this essay.
6. "Optimism—eller vad?" p. 276.
7. "Personligt dokument," *Ansikten* (Stockholm, 1932), p. 189.
8. *Ibid.*, p. 192.
9. For Johnson's memories of these meetings see "Minnesbild av en dag," *Stunder, vågor* (Stockholm, 1965), pp. 164–71.
10. "Personligt dokument," p. 194.
11. "På jakt efter källor," *Perspektiv på 30-talet* (Stockholm, 1961), p. 17.
12. "Personligt dokument," p. 195.
13. *Spår förbi Kolonos*, p. 253.
14. Carl Axel Westholm, "Skollärar Andersson, parlamentarismen och 'det ovanliga.' En studie kring Eyvind Johnsons *Stad i mörker*," *Ord och Bild*, LXVI (1957), 535–47.
15. *Perspektiv på 30-talet*, p. 22.
16. "Vändpunkt?" *Vintergatan* (1964), pp. 33–37.
17. *Perspektiv på 30-talet*, p. 22.
18. *Spår förbi Kolonos*, p. 9.
19. "Personligt dokument," p. 196.
20. "Mellan idyll och hemskhet," *Perspektiv på 30-talet*, p. 27.
21. "Hur hette dina hjältar, säg?" *BLM*, III (1934), 58.
22. *Perspektiv på 30-talet*, p. 26.
23. *Ibid.*, p. 29.
24. For a comparison between Johnson's life and his hero's, see Eyvind Johnson, "Om verkligheten i en roman," *Vintergatan* (1937), pp. 26–31; and Örjan Lindberger, "Enligt uppfattning."

25. "Författaren och friheten i det moderna samhället. En enquête,"
BLM, XVII (1948), 267.
26. See Åke Runnquist, "Ett handslag," *BLM*, XXIX (1960), 853–56.
27. Interview, *Dagens Nyheter*, December 7, 1943.
28. See Jarl Torbacke, "Krilon och verkligheten," *Dagens Nyheter*,
March 13, 1967; and *Krilon själv*, p. 465.
29. "En författare i sin tid . . ." *MLFÅ* (1962), p. 119.
30. Örjan Lindberger, "Eyvind Johnson och antiken," *Studiekamraten*,
XXXIX (1957), 195. Cf. *Tidens gång*, p. 296.
31. *Spår förbi Kolonos*, pp. 253–56.
32. *MLFÅ* (1962), p. 121.
33. E.g. *Vägar över Metaponto* (1959), on Italy; and *Spår förbi Kolonos*
(1961), on Greece.
34. Reprinted in an abridged form in *Stunder, vågor*.
35. A selection of these articles is reprinted in *Stunder, vågor*.
36. See Johan Falck, "Svall kring Nausikaa. Hur roman blev drama,"
Studiekamraten, XLIV (1962), 152–54.
37. "Diktaren—samhället," *SLT*, VIII (1945), 156.

Chapter Two

1. "Anteckningar om romanförfatteri," *Författaren och hans arbetsmetod. En enquête i "Dagens Nyheter,"* (Stockholm, 1950), p. 56.
2. "Eyvind Johnson," *Den 2. internasjonale studiekonferanse om nordisk litteratur* (Lillehammer, 1958), pp. 2–3.
3. "Romanens inbillade förfall," *Fronten*, I, No. 2 (1931), pp. 9–11;
"Romanens verkliga förfall," *Fronten*, I, No. 3 (1931), pp. 4–6; "Kring
några namn," *Fronten*, I, No. 4 (1931), pp. 4–6.
4. "Romanfunderingar," *Avsikter* (Stockholm, 1945), pp. 73–90.
5. "Den nya franska litteraturen," *Signalen*, August 5, 1926.
6. "Reflexioner kring André Gides sista roman," *Ny Tid*, September
9, September 20, October 14, 1927. I am indebted to Örjan Lindberger for
drawing my attention to these articles.
7. *Arbetet*, December 15, 1932.
8. Örjan Lindberger, "Eyvind Johnsons möte med Proust och Joyce,"
BLM, XXIX (1960), 555–56.
9. Lindberger, *op. cit.*, pp. 556–59. Story printed in *Dagens Nyheter*,
May 15, 1927.
10. *Les Faux-Monnayeurs* (Paris, 1925), p. 238.
11. "Eyvind Johnsons möte med Proust och Joyce," pp. 560–63.
12. Joseph Warren Beach, *The Twentieth Century Novel. Studies in Technique* (New York, 1932).
13. Beach, *op. cit.*, pp. 426–28.
14. Printed in *Stockholms-Tidningen*, January 27, 1929; reprinted in
Än en gång, kapten.

15. For an investigation of the use of stream of consciousness in *Kommentar*, see Gunnar Wiman, "Den inre monologen i Eyvind Johnsons roman *Kommentar till ett stjärnfall*," *MLFÅ* (1956), pp. 59–73.

16. Analyzed by Staffan Björck in *Romanens formvärld*, 5th ed. (Stockholm, 1963), p. 170.

Chapter Four

1. *Vinterresa i Norrbotten* (1955). Most easily obtainable in *Stunder, vågor*, p. 203.

2. "Anteckningar vid läsning i Gustav Hedenvind-Erikssons verk," *SLT*, II (1939), 155.

3. References are to volume and page. *Romantisk berättelse* is vol. I, while *Tidens gång* is vol. II.

Chapter Five

1. References are to volume and page. *Grupp Krilon* is vol. I, *Krilons resa* is vol. II, and *Krilon själv* vol. III.

2. *Dagens Nyheter*, December 7, 1943.

3. *Ibid.*

4. Erik Hjalmar Linder, *Ny illustrerad svensk litteraturhistoria*, V (Stockholm, 1952), p. 603.

5. C. A. Munk Nielsen, "Eyvind Johnson und Thomas Mann," *Orbis Litterarum*, XIII (1958), 27–43.

Chapter Six

1. For a more detailed survey see Örjan Lindberger, "Eyvind Johnson och antiken."

2. References to Xenophon's works are, within each title, to book (in roman) and chapter (in arabic).

3. See *Spår förbi Kolonos*, p. 255.

4. For a classicist's outraged comparison between Homer and Johnson, see Johannes Sundwall, "Homeros och Johnson," *Finsk tidskrift*, CXLI (1947), 164–75.

5. Sverker Göransson, "Berättartekniken i Eyvind Johnsons roman *Molnen över Metapontion*," *Samlaren*, LXXXIII (1962), 81.

6. Göransson, *op. cit.*, pp. 89–90.

7. Review in *Aftonbladet*, October 21, 1957.

8. "Boken som gömde sig," *Bokvännen*, XV (1960), 256–57.

9. See *Vägar över Metaponto* (1959), most easily available in *Stunder, vågor*.

Chapter Seven

1. For list of sources see interview in *Svenska Dagbladet*, September 14, 1949; and Yrjö Hirn, "En fransk häxeriprocess år 1634," *Den förgyllda balustraden* (Stockholm, 1953), pp. 103–23.

2. Aldous Huxley, *The Devils of Loudun*. London: Chatto and Windus, 1952.

3. For an analysis of the construction of *Hans nådes tid*, see A. Bolckmans, "Roman och film. Några funderingar kring Eyvind Johnsons roman *Hans nådes tid*," *Den sjätte internationella studiekonferensen över nordisk litteratur* (Uppsala, 1966), pp. 115–29.

4. In *Stunder, vågor*. E.g. pp. 278, 279, 283, 284, 289–91, 302.

5. "Blick på arbetsdagar," *Stunder, vågor*, p. 305. Johnson uses in particular the following volumes from *Die Geschichtschreiber der deutschen Vorzeit: Paulus Diakonus und die übrigen Geschichtschreiber der Langobarden* (Lieferung 6; Berlin, 1849); *Kaiser Karls Leben von Einhard* (Lieferung 8; Berlin, 1850); *Einhards Jahrbücher* (Lieferung 9; Berlin, 1850). For further information see Berndt Jonsson's unpublished *trebetygsuppsats* in Humanistiska biblioteket, University of Stockholm, entitled "Hans nådes tid—och Karl den stores. Studier i Eyvind Johnsons historiska roman *Hans nådes tid* och dess källor" (University of Stockholm, 1963).

6. "En författare i sin tid . . . " *MLFÅ* (1962), p. 119.

7. My discussion of this theme follows, with some change of emphasis, Bjarne Nygård, "Berättelsens makt och vanmakt," *Horisont* [Vasa], XI, No. 6 (1964), 19–22.

8. *Die Chronik Herimanns von Reichenau*, Die Geschichtscreiber der deutschen Vorzeit (Lieferung 15; Berlin, 1851).

9. *Jahrbücher von Genua*, Die Geschichtschreiber der deutschen Vorzeit (Lieferung 65; Leipzig, 1881).

10. *Aus Liudprands Werken*, Die Geschichtschreiber der deutschen Vorzeit (Lieferung 29; Berlin, 1853).

11. *Sächsische Geschichten*, Die Geschichtschreiber der deutschen Vorzeit (Lieferung 18; Berlin, 1852).

Chapter Eight

1. Staffan Björck, review in *Dagens Nyheter*, October 8, 1951.

2. See Staffan Björck, *Romanens formvärld*, 5th ed. (Stockholm, 1963), pp. 216–17.

3. Cf. *Spår förbi Kolonos*, p. 232.

Chapter Nine

1. E. M. Forster, *Aspects of the Novel*, London: Edward Arnold, 1927, ch. 2.

2. Göransson, *op. cit.,* pp. 72–73.
3. "Att hoppas, trots allt," *Röster i Radio,* XXVII, No. 52 (1960), p.14.
4. Some points in the next two paragraphs are discussed by Peter Hallberg in his article, "Eyvind Johnson, ordet och verkligheten," *BLM,* XXVII (1958), 538–48.

Selected Bibliography

PRIMARY SOURCES

A. Novels. (Published in Stockholm by Bonnier.)
Timans och rättfärdigheten (Timans and Justice). 1925.
Stad i mörker (Town in Darkness). 1927.
Stad i ljus (Town in Light). 1928
Minnas (Remembering). 1928.
Kommentar till ett stjärnfall (Commentary on a Falling Star). 1929.
Avsked till Hamlet (Farewell to Hamlet). 1930.
Bobinack. 1932.
Regn i gryningen (Rain at Dawn). 1933.
Nu var det 1914 (Now It Was 1914). 1934.
Här har du ditt liv (Here You Have Your Life). 1935.
Se dig inte om (Don't Look Back). 1936.
Slutspel i ungdomen (Finale in Youth). 1937.
Nattövning (Night Maneuvers). 1938.
Soldatens återkomst (The Soldier's Return). 1940.
Grupp Krilon (Krilon's Group). 1941.
Krilons resa (Krilon's Journey). 1942.
Krilon själv (Krilon Himself). 1943.
Strändernas svall (The Swell on the Beaches). 1946.
Drömmar om rosor och eld (Dreams of Roses and Fire). 1949.
Lägg undan solen (Put Away the Sun). 1951.
Romantisk berättelse (Romantic Tale). 1953.
Tidens gång (The Course of Time). 1955.
Molnen över Metapontion (The Clouds over Metapontion). 1957.
Hans nådes tid (The Days of His Grace). 1960.
Livsdagen lång (Life's Long Day). 1964.
Favel ensam (Favel Alone). 1968.

B. Collections of Short Stories.
De fyra främlingarna (The Four Strangers). Stockholm: Tiden, 1924.
Natten är här (The Night Has Come). Stockholm: Bonnier, 1932.
Än en gång, kapten (Once More, Captain). Stockholm: Bonnier, 1934.
Den trygga världen (The Secure World). Stockholm: Bonnier, 1940.
Pan mot Sparta (Pan against Sparta). Stockholm: Bonnier, 1946.

C. Plays

Strändernas svall (The Swell on the Beaches). Stockholm: Bonnier, 1948.

D. Journals, etc.

Dagbok från Schweiz (Diary from Switzerland). Stockholm: Bonnier, 1949.
Vinterresa i Norrbotten (Winter Journey in Norrbotten). Stockholm: Bonnier, 1955.
Vägar över Metaponto (Roads via Metaponto). Stockholm: Bonnier, 1959.
Spår förbi Kolonos (Traces past Colonos). Stockholm: Bonnier, 1961.
Stunder, vågor (Moments, Waves). Stockholm: Bonnier, 1965.

E. Articles.

"Den nya franska litteraturen" (The new French literature). *Signalen*, August 5, 1926.
"Reflexioner kring André Gides sista roman" (Reflections on André Gide's last novel). *Ny Tid*, September 9, September 20, October 14, 1927.
"Romanens inbillade förfall" (The imagined decline of the novel). *Fronten*, I, No. 2 (1931), 9–11.
"Romanens verkliga förfall" (The real decline of the novel). *Fronten*, I, No. 3 (1931), 4–6.
"Kring några namn" (Concerning some names). *Fronten*, I, No. 4 (1931), 4–6.
"Optimism—eller vad?" (Optimism—or what?). *Hågkomster och livsintryck*, XIII (Uppsala, 1932), 269–78.
"Personligt dokument" (Personal document). *Ansikten*. Stockholm: Bonnier, 1932, pp. 185–97.
Review of *Falskmyntarna (The Counterfeiters)* by André Gide. *Arbetet*, December 15, 1932.
"Om verkligheten i en roman" (On reality in a novel). *Vintergatan* (1937), pp. 26–31.
"Anteckningar vid läsning i Gustav Hedenvind-Erikssons verk" (Notes on reading Gustav Hedenvind-Eriksson's works). *Svensk litteraturtidskrift*, II (1939), 145–56.
Intervju om *Krilon, Dagens Nyheter*, December 7, 1943.
"Diktaren—samhället. Ett föredrag hållet i Oslo och Köpenhamn" (The writer—society. A lecture delivered in Oslo and Copenhagen). *Svensk litteraturtidskrift*, VIII (1945), 145–56.
"Romanfunderingar" (Thoughts about the novel). *Avsikter*. Stockholm: Bonnier, 1945, pp. 73–90.
"Författaren och friheten i det moderna samhället. En enquête" (The author and freedom in modern society. A questionnaire). *Bonniers Litterära Magasin*, XVII (1948), 266–67.

"Anteckningar om romanförfatteri" (Notes about novel writing). *För-fattaren och hans arbetsmetod, Dagens Nyheters* skriftserie. Stockholm: Bonnier, 1950, pp. 53–63.
"Boken som gömde sig" (The book that hid itself). *Bokvännen,* XV (1960), 256–57.
"Att hoppas, trots allt" (Hoping, despite everything). *Röster i Radio,* XXVII, No. 52 (1960), 14, 15, 63.
"En betraktares förutsättningar" (An observer's qualifications); "På jakt efter källor" (In search of sources); "Mellan idyll och hemskhet" (Between idyll and horror); "Ett decennium utan slut" (A decade without an end). *Perspektiv på 30-talet,* ed. Birger Christofferson and Thomas von Vegesack. Stockholm: Wahlström och Widstrand, 1961, pp. 9–39.
"'En författare i sin tid . . . ' (Ett kåseri)" (An author in his time). *Modersmålslärarnas Förenings Årsskrift* (1962), pp. 112–23.
"Vändpunkt?" (Turning point?). *Vintergatan* (1965), pp. 33–37.
"Möten" (Meetings). *Svensk Litteraturtidskrift,* XXIX (1966), 1–6.

F. Works in English Translation.
Return to Ithaca [Strändernas svall], transl. M. A. Michael. Preface by Mark Van Doren. London and New York: Thames and Hudson, 1952.
The Days of His Grace [Hans nådes tid], transl. Elspeth Harley Schubert. London: Chatto and Windus, 1968. New York: Vanguard Press.
1914 [Nu var det 1914], transl. Mary Sandbach. London: Adam Books, 1970.

SECONDARY SOURCES

BJÖRCK, STAFFAN. *Romanens formvärld* (The technical world of the novel). Stockholm: Natur och Kultur, 1953. Contains many excellent discussions of examples from Johnson's novels.
BOLCKMANNS, ALEX. "Roman och film. Några funderingar kring Eyvind Johnsons roman *Hans nådes tid*" (Novel and film. Some thoughts about Eyvind Johnson's novel *The Days of His Grace). Den sjätte internationella studiekonferensen över nordisk litteratur* (Uppsala, 1966). pp. 115–29. An analysis of the construction of *The Days of His Grace.*
CLAUDI, JÖRGEN. *Eyvind Johnson. En Karakteristik samt Bibliografi* (A characterization and bibliography). Copenhagen: Folmer Christensen, 1947. Rather superficial.
GÖRANSSON, SVERKER. "Berättartekniken i Eyvind Johnsons roman *Molnen över Metapontion*" (Narrative technique in Eyvind Johnson's novel *The Clouds over Metapontion). Samlaren,* LXXXIII (1962), 67–91. A useful technical analysis.
HALLBERG, PETER. "Eyvind Johnson, ordet och verkligheten" (Eyvind Johnson, the word and reality). *Bonniers Litterära Magasin,* XXVII

(1958), 538–48. Some good points in a confused mixture of Johnson the person and Johnson the author.

HIRN, YRJÖ. "En fransk häxeriprocess år 1634" (A French trial for witchcraft, 1634). *Den förgyllda balustraden.* Stockholm: Wahlström och Widstrand, 1953, pp. 103–23. On the historical background to *Dreams of Roses and Fire.*

LINDBERGER, ÖRJAN. "'Enligt uppfattning.' Om en roman av Eyvind Johnson och några protokollsböcker" ('As understood.' About a novel of Eyvind Johnson's and some minutes). *Nordisk tidskrift,* XXXIII (1957), 197–207. An account of Johnson's early political activities and their relevance to *The Novel About Olof.*

———"Eyvind Johnson." *Den 2. internasjonale studiekonferanse om nordisk litteratur* (Lillehammer, 1958), pp. 1–9. Discusses why Johnson should have become an experimenter with form in the novel.

———"Eyvind Johnson och antiken" (Eyvind Johnson and the Classical World). *Studiekamraten,* XXXIX (1957), 195–202. On Johnson's interest in classical literature and his retellings of it.

———"Eyvind Johnsons möte med Proust och Joyce" (Eyvind Johnson's meeting with Proust and Joyce). *Bonniers Litterära Magasin,* XXIX (1960), 554–63. An important and detailed study.

LINDER, ERIK HJALMAR. Article on Eyvind Johnson in *Fem decennier av nittonhundratalet,* II, *Ny illustrerad svensk litteraturhistoria.* Stockholm: Natur och Kultur, 1966, pp. 619–35. The standard literary history; places Johnson in context of Swedish literature.

NYGÅRD, BJARNE. "Berättelsens makt och vanmakt" (The power and impotence of a narrative). *Horisont* [Vasa], XI, No. 6 (1964), 19–22. An interesting study of *Life's Long Day.*

ORTON, GAVIN. "Eyvind Johnson—An Introduction." *Scandinavica,* V (1966), 111–23. A concentrated version of this book.

RUNNQUIST, ÅKE. "Ett handslag" (A handclasp). *Bonniers Litterära Magasin,* XXIX (1960), 583–86. An account of Johnson's work in this wartime newspaper.

SJÖBERG, LEIF. "Eyvind Johnson." *The American-Scandinavian Review,* LVI (1968), 369–78. A general article, in English, on the author and his work.

SUNDWALL, JOH. "Homeros och Johnson" (Homer and Johnson). *Finsk tidskrift,* CXLI (1947), 164–75. A comparison revealing strong moral disapproval of Johnson's way of treating Homer.

WESTHOLM, CARL AXEL. "Skollärar Andersson, parlamentarismen och 'det ovanliga.' En studie kring Eyvind Johnsons *Stad i mörker*" (Schoolmaster Andersson, parliamentarianism, and "the unusual." A study of Eyvind Johnson's *Town in Darkness*). *Ord och Bild,* LXVI (1957), 535–47. A good analysis both of the novel and of its connection with Johnson's political views.

WIMAN, GUNNAR. "Den inre monologen i Eyvind Johnsons roman

Kommentar till ett stjärnfall" (Stream of consciousness in Eyvind Johnson's novel *Commentary on a Falling Star*). *Modersmålslärarnas Förenings Årsskrift* (1956), pp. 59–73. A rather simplified treatment of the problem.

Index

159